Enjoying Birds in Michigan

A Guide and Resource Book for
Finding, Attracting and Studying Birds
In Michigan

Third Edition
Edited by
William L. Thompson

D0097090

Published by the
MICHIGAN AUDUBON SOCIETY
Revised, 1973

Kirtland's Warbler

Table of Contents

drawing by Robert S. Butsch

MOURNING WARBLER AND NODDING TRILLIUM

6

Introduction

William L. Thompson

This third edition of *Enjoying Birds in Michigan* is dedicated to all those who are just beginning the study of Michigan wildlife. It is intended to serve as an introduction to the birds of the state and to some of the most suitable places to look for birds and for other forms of wildlife, both animal and plant. Since the Michigan Audubon Society is devoted to increasing public awareness and understanding of our natural environment and of our native plants and animals it has seemed desirable to include in this little book some information about the society, its goals and activities.

The various chapters in the book are not intended to be exhaustive in their treatment of the various subjects, but rather they are written to lay a groundwork and to whet the appetite of the reader for future, more thorough study. We have not attempted to include such things as flowering plants, mosses or ferns, mammals, insects, etc., because to do so would require a much larger volume than is feasible at the present time. We do recognize the need for such a work, or series of works, devoted primarily to the Michigan flora and fauna, and for some years the society has been interested in the publication of a Michigan Naturalists' Handbook series. Until such time as this series becomes a reality, we hope that *Enjoying Birds in Michigan* and the various more comprehensive works listed in the section on books and periodicals will prove helpful.

— *Department of Biology, Wayne State University, Detroit, Michigan.*

Michigan Wildlife Calendar

by H. Lewis Batts, Jr.

SPRING is the season of bird migration, renewed plant growth, and the awakening of dormant amphibians, reptiles, and mammals. The plant world bursts into flower, resident birds and other animals begin their breeding activities, and migrants hasten to reach their summer homes. Growing vegetation provides cover, nesting material, and food for these animal activities. In spite of their apparent numbers, spring is the time of year when population levels of individual species are lowest and the time when adjustments are made from the maintenance activities of rather stable winter populations to the breeding activities of somewhat different populations.

March — Pussy willows greet early bird migrants arriving from farther south, and some winter residents may begin to move northward. Killdeers, Mourning Doves, kingfishers, Horned Larks, crows, and Starlings begin their nesting. Resident birds begin to modify their existing winter territories, if any, and to defend them more vigorously. The calls of Swamp Cricket Frogs and Spring Peepers resound above the intermittent ponds and marshes, and the waters of woodland pools may swarm with breeding salamanders.

April — Hepaticas and Skunk Cabbage herald the beginning of a new crop of wild flowers. The tempo of bird migration increases daily and additional species are nesting. Rails, early shorebirds, and most of the songbirds make their first appearance. The waterfowl migration reaches its peak in mid-April.

May — Spring wild flowers are in full array and new leaves are rapidly developing on the trees. Shorebird migration reaches its peak during the last week of this month. In general, the spring migration is at its height during May and the countryside rings with bird song. Bird baths and dripping or running water attract many birds to our yards and parks.

SUMMER is the season of proliferation in the natural world. Plants attain their annual growth and develop their seeds. Local animal population levels reach their peaks due to production of young. The number of spring migrants dwindles and the southward movement begins for those species which have completed their nesting. The larger frogs and toads sing and complete their breeding activity; and many salamanders leave their woodland pools and return to upland areas. Most mammals are taking advantage of the increased food supply in order to raise their offspring. This is the most popular season of the year for the wildlife observer but the heavy foliage often makes observation extremely difficult.

June — Bird nesting reaches its peak in this month due to a period of overlap between early and late-nesting species. Spring migration is practically over by the end of June; few birds are still migrating by then. Nest studies and animal photography are recommended projects.

July — Bird song is definitely lessened and young birds in juvenal plumage often confuse the observer. Autumn migration begins with the appearance of those shorebirds which have completed their nesting in the far north. The pace of May and June is slowed.

August — Local bird populations are at their highest point because the young of the year have fledged. The northward post-breeding migration of the Common Egret, Snowy Egret, and Little Blue Heron brings these visitors to our lakes and streams. The autumn shorebird migration increases in tempo, as the juvenile birds make their first appearance. Resident ducks are in eclipse plumage and may be seen among reeds and rushes along the shore. Masses of brightly colored late summer flowers give relief to the over-all browning of most of the herbaceous vegetation.

AUTUMN is the time of maturation. Plant growth gradually ceases; nuts, fruits, and seeds ripen; and leaves assume their autumn colors. In the animal world reproduction ceases and the widely scattered young have become independent of their parents. Birds and amphibians are much less vocal and seem to have disappeared; hibernating animals become more and more sluggish and quietly retire for their winter sleep. Many songbirds are flocking and some move southward. Autumn is a time of great fluctuation in local bird populations because of the almost daily arrival and departure of migrants — also a transition period from the breeding season of population increase to the winter season of struggle for mere existence of the individual.

September — Foliage is beginning to change to brighter colors and autumn flowers are blossoming. The general bird nesting season is over but a few late-nesting species may be still fledging young. The autumn shorebird migration is well under way. This and October are the peak months as far as actual bird numbers are concerned — many are in large flocks.

October — The autumn colors are at their best and "color tours" are in order. The shorebird migration has passed its peak but the waterfowl migration is gaining in intensity. Snow Buntings and Lapland Longspurs, the first winter visitors from the far north, may arrive and hibernating animals retire to their dens. Feeding stations should be placed and filled.

November — Trees still show traces of autumn color in the southern portion of the state but nearly all the leaves will fall by the end of the month. Most of the migrant songbirds have departed but warm weather may increase the number of stragglers. There is great activity among the waterfowl but freezing temperatures will force many of them south before winter is over.

WINTER is the season of dormancy — most plants lose their leaves and many die at least above ground level. Snow blankets the countryside, reducing food and cover for some animals and supplying protection for others. Animals that do not live beneath the snow at ground level are often forced to concentrate in areas where heavy protective cover is available. A fresh snowfall provides excellent opportunity for tracking and the study of animal trails may provide insight into behavior which cannot be secured in any other way. It is the season when local populations are reduced to the carrying capacity of the habitat available to them.

December — Most of the summer bird residents and the migrants have gone south and the permanent residents have modified their territories to winter size. The numbers of resident birds are augmented by the arrival of winter visitants from farther north. Feeding stations and the annual Christmas census are the highlights for observers during this month.

January — During the month the number of local birds may reach its lowest point of the year. Lakes and streams are frozen but Common Goldeneyes, mergansers, Black Ducks, and Canada Geese may be found wherever there is sufficient open water. Occasional invaders from the north such as Snowy Owls, Pine and Evening Grosbeaks, and the crossbills may be expected.

This is an excellent time to visit sanctuaries and other preserves which attract birds.

February — In the southern portions of the state the first of the migrating Eastern Bluebirds, Robins, and Red-winged Blackbirds make their appearance; bird song and other activity are on the increase. Some of the larger birds of prey have begun to nest. Breeding activities are conspicuous in tree squirrels and the first young may be born by the end of the month.

Now is a good time to clean and repair old nest boxes or to put out new ones.

— *Kalamazoo Nature Center, Kalamazoo, Michigan.*

A Check-List of Michigan Birds

by Harrison B. Tordoff

Any figure representing the number of bird species known to occur in Michigan is likely to be obsolete by the time it reaches print. At this writing in August, 1968, the total is 351. Inclusion in the accepted list is based on specimens or identifiable photographs, and therefore a few species undoubtedly occurring in the state are excluded for lack of tangible evidence (for example, Blue Grosbeak). Other species have been omitted because the birds reported are judged to have escaped from captivity (examples are the Asiatic Bar-headed Goose, American Flamingo, and South American Red-crested Cardinal). Decisions of this sort must be discretionary and will sometimes be wrong. Rigorous standards for admission to the state list should encourage bird students to obtain convincing evidence to back their reports of rarities. Careful, on the spot, field descriptions and photographs are particularly important. Records of rare birds as well as new information on distribution and nesting of common Michigan birds should be published in *The Jack-Pine Warbler* or sent to the Curator of Birds, Museum of Zoology, The University of Michigan, Ann Arbor, where permanent collections and files on Michigan birds are maintained.

In the following list, the symbols used are:

B — Breeding record for the state.

N — Most likely to be found *North* of a line from Bay City to Muskegon.

S — Most likely to occur *South* of this line. These distributional symbols refer primarily to breeding birds or winter visitants from the north.

R — Rare; fairly regular in appearance but in small numbers.

A — Accidental; five or fewer records for the state.

Order *Gaviiformes*
  Family *Gaviidae*
    __Common Loon, B N
    __Red-throated Loon, R
Order *Podicipediformes*
  Family *Podicipedidae*
    __Red-necked Grebe
    __Horned Grebe
    __Eared Grebe, A
    __Western Grebe, A
    __Pied-billed Grebe, B
Order *Pelecaniformes*
  Family *Pelecanidae*
    __White Pelican, R
  Family *Sulidae*
    __Gannet, A

Family *Phalacrocoracidae*
    __Double-crested
      Cormorant, B N

Order *Ciconiiformes*
  Family *Ardeidae*
    __Great Blue Heron, B
    __Green Heron, B
    __Little Blue Heron, S
    __Cattle Egret, R
    __Common Egret, B S
    __Snowy Egret, R S
    __Louisiana Heron, A
    __Black-crowned
      Night Heron, B

11

___Yellow-crowned
  Night Heron, R
___Least Bittern, B
___American Bittern, B
Family *Ciconiidae*
___Wood Ibis, A
Family *Threskiornithidae*
___Glossy Ibis, A
___White-faced Ibis, A

Order *Anseriformes*
Family *Anatidae*
___Mute Swan, B
___Whistling Swan
___Trumpeter Swan, A
___Canada Goose, B
___Brant, R
___White-fronted Goose, R
___Snow Goose
___Blue Goose
___Fulvous Tree Duck, A
___Mallard, B
___Black Duck, B
___Gadwall, B
___Pintail, B
___Green-winged Teal, B
___Blue-winged Teal, B
___Cinnamon Teal, A
___European Widgeon, R
___American Widgeon, B
___Shoveler, B
___Wood Duck, B
___Redhead, B
___Ring-necked Duck, B N
___Canvasback, B
___Greater Scaup, B
___Lesser Scaup, B
___Common Goldeneye, B
___Barrow's Goldeneye, A
___Bufflehead
___Oldsquaw
___Harlequin Duck, R
___King Eider, A
___Common Eider, A
___White-winged Scoter
___Surf Scoter
___Common Scoter, R

___Ruddy Duck, B
___Hooded Merganser, B
___Common Merganser, B N
___Red-breasted
  Merganser, B N

Order *Falconiformes*
Family *Cathartidae*
___Turkey Vulture, B
Family *Accipitridae*
___Swallow-tailed Kite, A
___Goshawk, B R N
___Sharp-shinned Hawk, B
___Cooper's Hawk, B
___Red-tailed Hawk, B
___Red-shouldered Hawk, B
___Broad-winged Hawk, B
___Swainson's Hawk, A
___Rough-legged Hawk
___Golden Eagle, R
___Bald Eagle, B
___Marsh Hawk, B
Family *Pandionidae*
___Osprey, B
Family *Falconidae*
___Gyrfalcon, A
___Peregrine Falcon, B R N
___Pigeon Hawk, B R N
___Sparrow Hawk, B

Order *Galliformes*
Family *Tetraonidae*
___Spruce Grouse, B N
___Ruffed Grouse, B
___Greater Prairie
  Chicken, B N
___Sharp-tailed Grouse, B N
Family *Phasianidae*
___Bobwhite, B S
___Ring-necked Pheasant, B
___Gray Partridge, B
Family *Meleagrididae*
___Turkey, B

Order *Gruiformes*
Family *Gruidae*
___Sandhill Crane, B
Family *Rallidae*

12

___King Rail, B S
___Virginia Rail, B
___Sora, B
___Yellow Rail, B N
___Black Rail, R
___Purple Gallinule, A
___Common Gallinule, B
___American Coot, B

Order *Charadriiformes*
Family *Charadriidae*
___Semipalmated Plover
___Piping Plover, B
___Killdeer, B
___American Golden Plover
___Black-bellied Plover
___Ruddy Turnstone
Family *Scolopacidae*
___American Woodcock, B
___Common Snipe, B
___Whimbrel, R
___Eskimo Curlew
   (perhaps extinct)
___Upland Plover, B
___Spotted Sandpiper, B
___Solitary Sandpiper
___Willet, R
___Greater Yellowlegs
___Lesser Yellowlegs
___Knot
___Purple Sandpiper, R
___Pectoral Sandpiper
___White-rumped Sandpiper
___Baird's Sandpiper
___Least Sandpiper
___Dunlin
___Short-billed Dowitcher
___Long-billed Dowitcher
___Stilt Sandpiper
___Semipalmated Sandpiper
___Western Sandpiper, R
___Buff-breasted Sandpiper, R
___Marbled Godwit, R
___Hudsonian Godwit, R
___Ruff, A
___Sanderling

Family *Recurvirostridae*
___American Avocet, R
Family *Phalaropodidae*
___Red Phalarope, R
___Wilson's Phalarope, B
___Northern Phalarope, R
Family *Stercorariidae*
___Pomarine Jaeger, A
___Parasitic Jaeger, R
___Long-tailed Jaeger, A
Family *Laridae*
___Glaucous Gull, R
___Iceland Gull, R
___Great Black-backed Gull
___Herring Gull, B
___California Gull, A
___Ring-billed Gull, B
___Black-headed Gull, A
___Laughing Gull, R
___Franklin's Gull, R
___Bonaparte's Gull
___Little Gull, R
___Black-legged Kittiwake, A
___Sabine's Gull, A
___Forster's Tern
___Common Tern, B
___Least Tern, R
___Caspian Tern, B N
___Black Tern, B
Family *Alcidae*
___Thick-billed Murre, R
___Dovekie, A
___Ancient Murrelet, A

Order *Columbiformes*
Family *Columbidae*
___Band-tailed Pigeon, A
___Mourning Dove, B
___Passenger Pigeon (extinct)
___Ground Dove, A

Order *Cuculiformes*
Family *Cuculidae*
___Yellow-billed Cuckoo, B
___Black-billed Cuckoo, B
___Groove-billed Ani, A

13

Order *Strigiformes*
  Family *Tytonidae*
  __Barn Owl, B R
  Family *Strigidae*
  __Screech Owl, B
  __Great Horned Owl, B
  __Snowy Owl, R
  __Hawk Owl, R N
  __Burrowing Owl, A
  __Barred Owl, B
  __Great Gray Owl, R N
  __Long-eared Owl, B
  __Short-eared Owl, B
  __Boreal Owl, R N
  __Saw-whet Owl, B

Order *Caprimulgiformes*
  Family *Caprimulgidae*
  __Whip-poor-will, B
  __Common Nighthawk, B

Order *Apodiformes*
  Family *Apodidae*
  __Chimney Swift, B
  __White-throated Swift, A
  Family *Trochilidae*
  __Ruby-throated
    Hummingbird, B

Order *Coraciiformes*
  Family *Alcedinidae*
  __Belted Kingfisher, B

Order *Piciformes*
  Family *Picidae*
  __Yellow-shafted Flicker, B
  __Pileated Woodpecker, B N
  __Red-bellied
  · Woodpecker, B S
  __Red-headed Woodpecker, B
  __Yellow-bellied
    Sapsucker, B
  __Hairy Woodpecker, B
  __Downy Woodpecker, B
  __Black-backed Three-toed
    Woodpecker, B N
  __Northern Three-toed
    Woodpecker, B R N

Order *Passeriformes*
  Family *Tyrannidae*
  __Eastern Kingbird, B
  __Western Kingbird, B R
  __Scissor-tailed Flycatcher, A
  __Great Crested Flycatcher, B
  __Eastern Phoebe, B
  __Yellow-bellied
    Flycatcher, B N
  __Acadian Flycatcher, B S
  __Traill's Flycatcher, B
  __Least Flycatcher, B
  __Eastern Wood Pewee, B
  __Olive-sided Flycatcher, B N
  Family *Alaudidae*
  __Horned Lark, B
  Family *Hirundinidae*
  __Tree Swallow, B
  __Bank Swallow, B
  __Rough-winged Swallow, B
  __Barn Swallow, B
  __Cliff Swallow, B
  __Purple Martin, B
  Family *Corvidae*
  __Gray Jay, B N
  __Blue Jay, B
  __Black-billed Magpie, A
  __Common Raven, B N
  __Common Crow, B
  Family *Paridae*
  __Black-capped Chickadee, B
  __Carolina Chickadee, A
  __Boreal Chickadee, B N
  __Tufted Titmouse, B S
  Family *Sittidae*
  __White-breasted Nuthatch, B
  __Red-breasted Nuthatch, B N
  Family *Certhiidae*
  __Brown Creeper, B
  Family *Troglodytidae*
  __House Wren, B
  __Winter Wren, B N
  __Bewick's Wren, B R S
  __Carolina Wren, B S
  __Long-billed Marsh Wren, B
  __Short-billed Marsh Wren, B

—Rock Wren, A
Family *Mimidae*
—Mockingbird, B R
—Catbird, B
—Brown Thrasher, B
Family *Turdidae*
—Robin, B
—Varied Thrush, R
—Wood Thrush, B
—Hermit Thrush, B N
—Swainson's Thrush, B N
—Gray-cheeked Thrush
—Veery, B
—Eastern Bluebird, B
—Townsend's Solitaire, A
Family *Sylviidae*
—Blue-gray Gnatcatcher, B S
—Golden-crowned
  Kinglet, B N
—Ruby-crowned Kinglet, B N
Family *Motacillidae*
—Water Pipit
—Sprague's Pipit, A
Family *Bombycillidae*
—Bohemian Waxwing, R
—Cedar Waxwing, B
Family *Laniidae*
—Northern Shrike
—Loggerhead Shrike, B
Family *Sturnidae*
—Starling, B
Family *Vireonidae*
—White-eyed Vireo, R S
—Bell's Vireo, A
—Yellow-throated Vireo, B
—Solitary Vireo, B N
—Red-eyed Vireo, B
—Philadelphia Vireo
—Warbling Vireo, B
Family *Parulidae*
—Black-and-white
  Warbler, B
—Prothonotary Warbler, B S
—Worm-eating Warbler, R
—Golden-winged
  Warbler, B

—Blue-winged
  Warbler, B S
—Tennessee Warbler, B N
—Orange-crowned Warbler
—Nashville Warbler, B N
—Parula Warbler, B N
—Yellow Warbler, B
—Magnolia Warbler, B N
—Cape May Warbler, B N
—Black-throated
  Blue Warbler, B N
—Myrtle Warbler, B N
—Audubon's Warbler, A
—Black-throated
  Gray Warbler, A
—Black-throated
  Green Warbler, B N
—Cerulean Warbler, B S
—Blackburnian Warbler, B N
—Yellow-throated
  Warbler, B R S
—Chestnut-sided Warbler, B
—Bay-breasted Warbler
—Blackpoll Warbler
—Pine Warbler, B
—Kirtland's Warbler, B N
—Prairie Warbler, B N
—Palm Warbler, B N
—Ovenbird, B
—Northern Waterthrush, B
—Louisiana Waterthrush, B S
—Kentucky Warbler, R
—Connecticut Warbler, B R N
—Mourning Warbler, B
—Yellowthroat, B
—Yellow-breasted Chat, B S
—Hooded Warbler, B R S
—Wilson's Warbler
—Canada Warbler, B
—American Redstart, B
Family *Ploceidae*
—House Sparrow, B
Family *Icteridae*
—Bobolink, B
—Eastern Meadowlark, B
—Western Meadowlark, B

15

___Yellow-headed
    Blackbird, B R
___Red-winged Blackbird, B
___Orchard Oriole, B S
___Baltimore Oriole, B
___Rusty Blackbird, B N
___Brewer's Blackbird, B
___Common Grackle, B
___Brown-headed Cowbird, B
Family *Thraupidae*
___Scarlet Tanager, B
___Summer Tanager, R
Family *Fringillidae*
___Cardinal, B
___Rose-breasted Grosbeak, B
___Black-headed Grosbeak, A
___Indigo Bunting, B
___Painted Bunting, A
___Dickcissel, B
___Evening Grosbeak, B N
___Purple Finch, B N
___Pine Grosbeak
___Hoary Redpoll, R N
___Common Redpoll
___Pine Siskin, B N
___American Goldfinch, B
___Red Crossbill, B N

___White-winged Crossbill, B N
___Rufous-sided Towhee, B
___Lark Bunting, A
___Savannah Sparrow, B
___Grasshopper Sparrow, B
___Le Conte's Sparrow, B R N
___Henslow's Sparrow, B S
___Sharp-tailed Sparrow, R
___Vesper Sparrow, B
___Lark Sparrow, B R S
___Bachman's Sparrow, A
___Slate-colored Junco, B N
___Oregon Junco, R
___Tree Sparrow
___Chipping Sparrow, B
___Clay-colored Sparrow, B N
___Field Sparrow, B
___Harris' Sparrow, R
___White-crowned Sparrow
___White-throated
    Sparrow, B N
___Fox Sparrow
___Lincoln's Sparrow, B N
___Swamp Sparrow, B
___Song Sparrow, B
___Smith's Longspur, A
___Lapland Longspur
___Snow Bunting

_____   _____

_____   _____

_____   _____

_____   _____

_____   _____

_____   _____

_____   _____

_____   _____

_____   _____

_____   _____

— *Museum of Zoology, University of Michigan, Ann Arbor, Michigan.*

100 Common Michigan Birds

by Homer D. Roberts

COMMON LOON *Gavia immer* 28"-36"

The Loon is one of our largest diving birds. Unable to walk well or take off from land, it builds its nest on vegetation within a foot or two of water. Two dark greenish eggs are laid, often only one maturing. Loons live almost entirely on fish, which they catch by superb diving and underwater swimming. They often submerge from view as does a submarine, only to reappear a great distance from the original spot. Loons have several calls, the best known resembling clear melancholy laughter. The breeding plumage is black with checkered back and white breast. In winter, when the bird is in the Gulf Coast region, it is largely gray.

PIED-BILLED GREBE *Podilymbus podiceps* 12"-15"

The Pied-billed Grebe, or helldiver, is our smallest grebe, and is found in lakes, streams and ponds. An expert diver, it prefers to excape danger by diving rather than by flight. It is a gray-brown bird with a black throat band, and often rides very low in the water. The Pied-bill is easily distinguished from other species by its thick, chicken-like bill encircled by a black band. A floating nest of decaying vegetation is built, on which are laid five to seven light-colored eggs. Food consists of insects, crayfish and small fish. The Pied-bill's call is a cuckoo-like "Cow-cow-cow-cow-cow."

GREAT BLUE HERON *Ardea herodias* 42"-52"

The Great Blue Heron is our largest wading bird. The plumage is slaty-blue, and it wears a dark head plume. It may be seen standing or walking slowly along edges of ponds or streams in search of small fish, frogs, crayfish, snakes and insects. An extremely wary bird, it seldom tolerates close approach. The bulky cumulative nest of sticks and twigs, containing four or five bluish eggs, is found in colonies high in wooded swamps. While in flight, herons are easily distinguished from cranes, as their necks are doubled back into their shoulders while the cranes' necks extend out fully. The call of the Great Blue is a gutteral croak. Wintering occurs southward, usually in the Gulf states.

GREEN HERON *Butorides virescens* 16"-22"

Commonest and most widely distributed of the small herons is our Green Heron, resident of ponds, marshes, swamps and wooded streams. From a distance or in poor light the little "Fly-up-the-creek" appears black, but the greenish-yellow or orange legs are distinctive. When in flight it resembles the Crow, but with slower wing beats. Alarmed, the Green Heron raises its crest and nervously jerks its tail. The nest is a platform of sticks in a bush or tree, containing 3 to 6 pale blue eggs. Although often considered a solitary bird, the Green Heron sometimes nests in small colonies. Typical of herons, it eats small fish, crayfish and insects. The voice is a deep harsh "Kyaw!"

AMERICAN BITTERN Botaurus lentiginosus 23"-34"

The American Bittern, a "hermit" member of the heron family who rarely ventures out of the marsh, is better known for his unique song than for his appearance. Such nicknames as "thunder pumper" and "stake driver" help describe the unusual sounds of this chunky brown marsh dweller. Equally interesting is the bird's habit of "freezing," bill pointed to the sky, thus blending almost miraculously into his brown, reedy habitat. Four to 7 fuzzy young, sitting on the platform nest a few inches above the water, employ the same ruse to avoid detection. Frogs and other small marsh creatures make up the diet. American Bitterns winter from central United States to Central America.

CANADA GOOSE Branta canadensis 25"-43"

Best known of all geese is the large Canada Goose, or "honker," whose dramatic spring and fall flights are universal symbols of the mysteries of migration. Winging noisily northward in great wavering V formations or long lines, they are truly harbingers of spring. Their long black necks and white throat patches are distinctive field marks. Canada Geese are largely vegetarians, feeding on underwater plants or grazing in grassy marshes and stubble fields. Some insects are eaten. The nest, usually on high ground in marshes or near lakes, is made of grasses, twigs and reeds, lined with down. Five to 8 dull greenish or yellowish to buffy eggs are laid. Canada Geese usually mate for life.

MALLARD Anas platyhynchos 20"-28"

Mallards are shallow-water ducks, procuring their aquatic plant food by dabbling. They also seek grain in stubble fields long distances from water. Mallards are fairly large ducks, and are considered a table delicacy. The male is beautiful in its varied plumage of green head, rufous breast, gray and brown body, and purple-blue speculum. The female is much less conspicuous in her drab dress of brown. The feather-lined nest of grasses is found on the ground in tall vegetation near water, and contains eight to twelve buffy or olive-green eggs. The Mallard is one of the most abundant of all ducks. They winter from the Great Lakes south to the Gulf of Mexico.

BLACK DUCK Anas rubripes 21"-25"

The Black Duck is a close relative of the mallard, and its habits are similar. As a result of being sought after by hunters, it is one of the wildest and wariest of the ducks. It is really not black, but dark sooty brown, the sexes being similar. In flight its dark body and whitish wing linings are good identification marks. The bill is greenish yellow and the feet brownish red. Blacks are dabbling ducks, feeding upon aquatic plants and insects. The nest, containing six to twelve buff or cream eggs, is built of grasses on the ground, sometimes far from water. Black Ducks winter from the Great Lakes south to the Gulf of Mexico.

BLUE-WINGED TEAL *Anas discors* 15"-16"

The little Blue-winged Teal shows a preference for marshes, sluggish streams and grassy ponds, near which its down-lined nest is made. Here ten to twelve pale olive-buff eggs are laid. Blue-wings are not wary, and are therefore shot in great numbers. Besides its small size and dull coloration, other identifying characteristics of the male are its white crescent on either side of the face, pale blue patch on the leading edge of the wing, and green speculum. The female is similar but lacks the crescent face markings. The Blue-wing is a surface feeder, eating aquatic plants, mollusks, and insects. Wintering is from the Gulf region southward.

WOOD DUCK *Aix sponsa* 17"-20"

No other duck is so distinctly American as the beautifully-colored Wood Duck. The species lives and migrates mainly in the United States, although it breeds north to southern Canada and sometimes winters as far south as Mexico. The brilliant iridescence of the crested male and the large eye ring of the female make identification unmistakable. As the name indicates, the "Woodie" is a bird of the forested bottom lands and wooded streams. Nesting in a hollow tree or nest box, often high above the water, they lay 8 to 15 buffy white eggs. When old enough, the tiny ducklings "bail out," dropping uninjured to the water below. Wood Ducks are completely protected by law.

CANVASBACK *Aythya valisineria* 20"-24"

One of the largest of our ducks, the Canvasback is highly regarded among hunters as a table delicacy. Although it feeds chiefly on such aquatic vegetation as wild celery and pond weeds, the "Can" will eat fish and shellfish when necessary. The Canvasback is easily recognized by its large white areas, its rusty head, black breast, and its distinctive long sloping profile. Breeding in the prairie regions of western Canada and in the states just south of this area, the Canvasback migrates south in long lines or V-shaped flocks. The nest is built on a platform of marsh vegetation in shallow water. Ten or more gray-green eggs are laid.

SCAUP DUCKS *Aythya marila* (17"-20") and *Aythya affinis* (15"-18")

The Scaups are diving ducks and are usually found in large flocks, called rafts, on open bodies of water. There are two species, the Greater and Lesser, which are practically indistinguishable in the wild. As the name implies the Greater is larger and it has a greenish head, while the Lesser has a purplish head. From a distance they look black at both ends and white in the middle. The females of both species are brown with a conspicuous white mask at the base of the bill. Scaups are omnivorous, with a preference for mollusks and pond weeds. They breed from the Arctic to southern Canada and winter from the Great Lakes through Central America.

COMMON GOLDENEYE *Bucephala clangula* 17"-23"

A familiar winter sight on open water in our Great Lakes region is the hardy Goldeneye, who often remains all winter if waters are unfrozen. The best identification is the round white spot between the eye and the bill. Also, the bird shows much white on its body, and has a dark head. The Goldeneye's nickname of "whistler" is derived from the loud high-pitched whistling of the wings in flight. Like the Wood Duck, the Goldeneye often seeks a nesting site in a tree or rock cavity over or near water, where 12 to 15 pale green eggs are laid. When they are old enough, the young plummet uninjured to the ground or water.

COMMON MERGANSER *Mergus merganser* 22"-27"

An unforgettable sight is that of the Common Merganser taking off from water, using both wings and long running surface strides to launch itself into the air. An excellent swimmer and diver, the "Fishduck," as the Merganser is often called, lives chiefly on small fish caught below the surface. Long condemned for eating fish, the Merganser may actually be performing a valuable service by cutting down overpopulations of runt fish from our lakes. Common Mergansers nest in tree cavities, among rocks, or on the ground, producing from 6 to 17 creamy buff eggs. The breeding range is Canada and the northern edge of the United States. The birds winter from the Great Lakes to the Gulf.

TURKEY VULTURE *Cathartes aura* 30"-35"

The Turkey Vulture, or buzzard, is a black-bodied bird with six-foot wing-spread and a featherless red head. It lives almost entirely on dead animals which, from a sanitation standpoint, makes it one of our most valuable birds. It can be seen circling high in the air on almost motionless wings for long periods of time, the wings held above the horizontal to form a distinct "V." Vultures have keen eyesight, and not only watch the ground but constantly watch each other's movements as well. The nest, often hidden on the ground, in hollow stumps or rock cavities contains two white eggs. Our Vultures winter from the Ohio valley southward.

RED-TAILED HAWK *Buteo jamaicensis* 19"-25"

Red-tailed Hawks are among those misunderstood birds of prey which are often called "Chicken Hawks." All too often they suffer for the feeding habits of the smaller Cooper's and Sharp-shinned hawks, which do occasionally capture poultry. The Red-tail lives on small mammals, reptiles and a few birds. The name "Red-tail" refers to the rufous-red upper surface of the tail. The bird will sit for long periods on a perch, and because of its large size is an easy target for thoughtless or misinformed hunters. The Red-tailed Hawk and all other hawks are completely protected in Michigan. The nest, high in a tree in a wooded area, contains 2 or 3 dull white eggs spotted with brown.

BALD EAGLE *Haliaeetus leucocephalus* 30″-34″

The Bald Eagle, our national emblem, is a majestic bird, fully protected by state and federal law. The adult is brown with white head and tail, but the white may not appear until the third or fourth year. Eagles soar on horizontal wings of 6 to 7½ foot spread. Since food consists chiefly of fish, the bald eagle is usually seen near bodies of water. It frequently eats dead fish washed ashore, or steals a catch from the osprey. The huge cumulative nest of sticks, usually in the main fork of a high tree, is used year after year. One to four white eggs are laid. The Eagle's voice is an unregal, harsh cackle. They winter near ice-free water.

MARSH HAWK *Circus cyaneus* 18″-24″

The Marsh Hawk, or Harrier, is a bird of the open country, and can be seen flying low over farm lands or marshes in search of mice, frogs, insects and occasional birds. It is easily recognized in flight by the white rump patch as well as the manner in which the wings are held above the horizontal. The female is considerably larger than the male, and has a streaked brown plumage, while the male is gray. Marsh Hawks nest on grassy hummocks in marshes, laying four to six bluish-white eggs. As with other hawks, incubation begins with the laying of the first egg, resulting in various-sized young in the nest. While some individuals remain through the winter, southward migration is more common.

AMERICAN KESTREL *Falco sparverius* 9″-10″

The Sparrow Hawk, or Kestrel, is the smallest and most colorful hawk in North America. It can often be seen perched on a telephone wire, or hovering in mid-air on long-pointed wings, ready to pounce on a mouse, grasshopper, or small reptile. The Sparrow Hawk is about Robin size and is a true falcon. The blue-gray wings of the male, the rufous back and tail, and the black and white face markings are distinctive. The female is slightly larger but less colorful. The four to seven white or buff eggs, brown speckled, are placed in a hollow tree or nest box. The call is a rapid "Killy-killy-killy!" Sparrow Hawks remain here through the winter.

RUFFED GROUSE *Bonasa umbellus* 16″-19″

The Ruffed Grouse is a large red-brown or gray-brown chicken-like bird of the woodlands. Although largely a vegetarian, eating fruits, buds, seeds and nuts, it also consumes many insects. As a game bird the Ruffed Grouse, or Partridge, furnishes a great deal of sport. One of its well-known characteristics is the drumming made by the male beating the air with its wings during courtship. It begins with a loud tattoo which starts slowly as if measured, then quickens, and finally settles into a whirring rumble. The nest, containing from seven to seventeen whitish eggs, is built on the ground and is subject to much predation. Ruffed Grouse are permanent residents.

21

BOBWHITE *Colinus virginianus* 8½"-10½"

The Bobwhite is one of the best known American game birds. A permanent resident, it is a chicken-like bird no larger than a meadowlark. Its cheery call of "Bob, bobwhite!" can be heard as one walks through meadows or brushy areas. A covey of quail will roost on the ground tail to tail with their heads pointing outward, ready to explode into the air should danger approach. Their nests, containing ten to twenty white eggs, are built of grasses on the ground along brushy borders of fields. To the farmer and orchardist the Bobwhite's insect-eating habits make it an extremely valuable ally. Weed seeds and small grains are also eaten.

RING-NECKED PHEASANT *Phasianus colchicus* 33"-36" (male)

The Ring-necked Pheasant, imported from Asia in the 1880's, is our largest upland game bird. The male is unmistakable with its iridescent plumage, white neckrings, and long pointed tail. The female is a brownish bird with a pointed though much shorter tail. Though the Pheasant does some damage to farm crops, it also does much good by destroying insects and weed seeds. It also eats wild fruits and berries. Ten to sixteen, olive-colored eggs are placed in a nest on the ground in tall meadow grasses. Grass fires and early mowing cause enormous losses to eggs and incubating females. The male's call is a loud double squawk, something like the crowing of a young bantam rooster.

SORA *Porzana carolina* 8"-10"

During summer months Sora Rails may be found in wet meadows and in fresh-water marshes. Their protective coloration and secretive ways are such that they might easily be passed by were it not for their clear call of "Ker-wee!" or their rolling, descending whinny. They prefer to slip through the reeds rather than fly to escape danger. The Sora can be recognized by its short chicken-like bill, black face and throat, brown back and barred flanks. They are fond of wild rice, weed seeds, small crustaceans and insects. The nest is of swamp vegetation placed on the ground in marshes, and contains six to sixteen buffy eggs, spotted with brown. Soras winter from southern United States to South America.

COOT *Fulica americana* 13"-16"

Coots are often observed with ducks in marshes, ditches and on open water. They swim with a peculiar pumping motion and, when rising from the water, patter their scalloped feet on the surface for many steps before taking to the air. The plumage is a dark slate color, with the head and neck nearly black. The bill is a contrasting white. Coots feed upon aquatic plants and insects and small crustaceans. The nest of grasses is located on platforms of reeds and rushes in marshes, and contains six to fifteen buffy-white eggs, thickly speckled with brown. The call is a guttural cackling. Coots winter south to the Gulf of Mexico.

KILLDEER *Charadrius vociferus* 9"-11"

One is almost certain to find the Killdeer in meadows, newly-plowed fields, mud-flats and along sandy shores. It can be readily identified by its two breast bands, its cinnamon-brown rump, and its oft-repeated call of "Kill-dee! kill-dee! kill-dee!" It builds almost no nest, but simply hollows out a shallow depression and lines it with small stones and grasses. Here four large creamy-white eggs, spotted with brown, are laid. Killdeers are noted for their habit of feigning a broken leg or wing, and luring the intruder from the nest. Killdeers are extremely valuable, living almost entirely on injurious insects. They arrive very early in the spring from their southern United States winter quarters.

AMERICAN WOODCOCK *Philohela minor* 10"-12"

The Woodcock inhabits boggy ravines in moist woodlands, living largely on worms which it probes from the soft earth with its long sensitive bill. The Woodcock is noted for its mating song and flight. The song begins on the ground, and may continue several hundred feet into the air. Louder and shriller sounds the wing-song, until after a short pause, the bird pitches head-long in a zig-zag fashion to the earth again. The nest of leaves and grasses is on the ground at the wood's edge, and contains four buffy eggs, spotched with brown. The Woodcock's "dead-leaf" coloration is so perfect that the female will often allow one to approach the nest and touch her, thinking herself to be unnoticed.

COMMON SNIPE *Capella gallinago* 10"-11"

A most startling experience on a walk through a low meadow or marshy field is the sudden "explosion" of a Snipe. Winging away in a crazy zig-zag flight and uttering a rasping nasal note, the "jack snipe" offers a poor target for either photographer or hunter. The Common Snipe has a long slender bill, an ideal adaptation for probing for aquatic larvae, snails or earthworms. It also eats grasshoppers and beetles. One of the weird sounds of spring is the vibrant whistling or "winnowing" sound produced by the feathers during mating display flights. The nest, a shallow depression lined with grasses, contains 3 to 4 pale brown eggs blotched with darker brown.

SPOTTED SANDPIPER *Actitis macularia* 7"-8"

The Spotted Sandpiper is one of the most common shore birds. "Spotties" are often seen in pairs or small groups. As they feed along the shores and marshes they are continually teetering and uttering the familiar "Peet-weet!" These characteristics, plus the dark spots on the white underparts, make identification easy. When disturbed, they fly just above the water with low, quivering wingbeats, making a wide arc to alight farther down the shore. Food consists of insects, worms and small crustaceans. The nest, hidden in vegetation on the ground near water, contains four large creamy-white eggs heavily mottled with brown. Incubation and care of the young are performed by the male. Like other precocial birds, the young leave the nest soon after hatching.

23

HERRING GULL *Larus argentatus* 23″-26″

The Herring Gull, often called sea gull, is one of our commonest large gulls and is the one usually seen about harbors, or following in the wake of a streamer. It is a handsome bird with its pearl-gray back, white head and under-parts, black wingtips, and pink legs. As a scavanger it renders great service in keeping harbors and beaches free from decaying fish and other refuse. Herring Gulls nest on the ground, usually in colonies on islands of the Great Lakes. The immature of this species is dark brownish-slate throughout, and takes three years to attain adult plumage. Herring Gulls winter from the Great Lakes to the Gulf.

RING-BILLED GULL *Larus delawarensis* 18″-20″

Like the larger Herring Gull which it so closely resembles, the Ring-billed Gull is a scavanger, following ships, patrolling beaches for dead fish, and frequenting garbage dumps. They are often seen inland, following the plow for worms. Besides the smaller size, other good field marks are the ringed bill and the yellowish or greenish legs. Ring-bills are gregarious birds, nesting in colonies on the ground on small islands. Usually 3 buffy eggs are laid, irregularly blotched with brown. Immature Ring-billed Gulls are lighter in color than young Herring Gulls, and display a dark, distinct tail band. They winter from the Great Lakes south.

COMMON TERN *Sterna hirundo* 13″-16″

This dainty little "sea swallow" is often seen flying gracefully over sandy beaches and about harbors in summer. It can easily be recognized by its white and pearl-gray body, black cap, black-tipped coral bill, and orange feet. In flight its long pointed wings and deeply forked tail aid in identification. Common Terns feed on small fishes, or aquatic insects which they catch by swooping down to the water. They nest in colonies along sandy beaches and on small islands off shore. The nest, merely a shallow depression lined with some vegetation, contains three to four olive-gray to buff eggs, heavily marked with chocolate brown. The winter home of the Common Tern is from Florida southward.

BLACK TERN *Chlidonias niger* 9″-10″

The Black Tern is a common water bird, and a summer resident of marshes, sloughs and wet meadows. The entire head and underparts are black; the back and wings are gray; and the under tail coverts are white. It is a dainty, graceful little creature, but can prove very aggressive if its nest is approached. It utters a shrill, angry cry as it strikes at the intruder again and again. The nest is placed on marsh vegetation, often floatings, or on an old muskrat home. Two or three buff to brown eggs, chocolate marked are laid. The Black Tern is chiefly insectivorous. It winters in South America.

24

MOURNING DOVE *Zenaida macroura* 11"-13"

The Mourning Dove gets its name from its doleful song of "Coo-o-o, coo-oo, coo-oo." Returning to the northern states in early spring, it is often found in stubble fields searching for fallen grain. A considerable number remain here all winter, and frequently visit feeding stations. The Mourning Dove's nest, containing two white eggs, is very poorly constructed of twigs, rootlets and grasses. The young are fed on "pigeon's milk," secreted by the parents. While in flight the wings of the Mourning Dove create a strange musical vibration, the sound somewhat resembling the metallic ring of a taut steel wire. Its food consists chiefly of weed seeds and waste grains.

YELLOW-BILLED CUCKOO *Coccyzus americanus* 11"-13"

Although fairly common in Michigan, the shy and retiring Yellow-billed Cuckoo is not generally well-known. It's call, a rapid throaty "Ka-ka-ka-kowp-kowp-kowp!" is often associated with impending rain, giving rise to the nickname of "Rain Crow." A voracious eater of hairy caterpillars, the Cuckoo is a valuable asset to forest, orchard and garden. The nest is a poor platform of small leaf-lined twigs, on which are laid 3 to 5 pale green eggs. Our Cuckoos are both long, slender, brown above and white below; however, the Yellow-billed Cuckoo can be distinguished from the Black-billed Cuckoo by the rufous shading of its flight feathers. Cuckoos winter in South America.

BARN OWL *Tyto alba* 15"-20"

Nature abundantly equipped the Barn Owl for its nocturnal job of hunting mice and other small mammals. The keen eyes, sensitive ears, soft plumage and fringed wing feathers enable it to detect and capture its prey with ease. The Barn Owl, or "Monkey-faced Owl" as it is frequently called, prefers to hide out in barns, old towers and belfries, and is seldom observed even in its common range. It is a resident from southern Michigan on south. Like others of its kind, the Barn Owl regurgitates the undigestible bones, fur or feathers of its prey, and these "pellets" provide excellent proof of their useful food habits.

SCREECH OWL *Otus asio* 8"-10"

The Screech Owl sometimes resembles a ball of feathers, as broad as it is long, but can stretch itself tall and thin when it wants to. It can be found in both the red and gray color phases, regardless of age or sex. The cry is a quivering, tremulous wail, running down the scale. Screech Owls nest in holes in trees, and will even use large nest boxes. Three to five white eggs are laid. With its keen eyesight and noiseless flight it searches for its prey at night. Its fondness for mice and large insects makes it extremely useful, and every effort should be made to protect it. Screech Owls are permanent residents in Michigan.

25

GREAT HORNED OWL *Bubo virginianus* 18"-23"

The Great Horned Owl is one of the largest and most powerful of the birds of prey. It has a conspicuous pair of ear tufts, and its large yellow eyes are constantly alert for prey. It is not a friendly bird, and will hiss and snap its bill viciously when cornered. The white throat band is distinctive. This bird is sometimes destructive to birds, but its diet usually consists of rabbits, rats, mice, gophers and other destructive animals. It chiefly inhabits heavily forested areas. The nest, located in an old hawk or crow nest, hollow tree, or even on the ground, contains two or three white eggs. The call of the Great Horned Owl is a series of deep monotonous hoots, usually five in number. It is a permanent resident.

COMMON NIGHTHAWK *Chordeiles minor* 8"-10"

The Nighthawk is not really a hawk, but an insectivorous bird related to the Whip-poor-will. Arriving in late May from South America they are easily identified by their long, sharply-pointed wings marked by a distinct white patch. Nighthawks zoom, glide and dive as they catch insects on the wing. Their call is a nasal "Peent" uttered in flight, but they are frequently heard with an almost explosive "Zoomp" as they pull out of their dives. At rest the Nighthawk sits lengthwise on a limb. Though formerly nesting on the ground, the Nighthawk has adapted itself well to civilization and is frequently found nesting on gravel rooftops, where it lays two dull-white eggs, speckled with brown.

CHIMNEY SWIFT *Chaetura pelagica* 5"-6"

The Chimney Swift is a familiar sight as its streamlined form swiftly soars and circles in the air while feeding on winged insects. Sooty black in color, it is characterized by long stiff wings and the appearance of no tail. As it flits about on quivering wings, it emits a high-pitched chippering sound. The platform-like nest is glued together with a secretion from the mouth and fastened to the inside wall of a chimney, abandoned well, or old barn. Four to five tiny, white eggs are laid. The tail feathers of the Swift are equipped with sharply pointed quills which help it to hang onto the bricks. The bird winters in Peru.

RUBY-THROATED HUMMINGBIRD
Archilochus colubris 3"-4"

The Hummingbird is the smallest Michigan bird. Both sexes are metallic green above, but the male sports a glowing red throat. It is often seen among our garden flowers drinking nectar from the blossoms. When feeding, it inserts its long bill deep into the flower while hovering on rapidly-whirring wings. The Hummingbird also consumes many small creatures such as plant lice and small spiders. The very small nest of plant down, bound together with spider web, is covered with lichens and saddled on a limb. Two miniature white eggs are laid. The Hummingbird is often confused with the sphinx moth, which it somewhat resembles. Wintering occurs from Florida southward.

BELTED KINGFISHER *Megaceryle alcyon* 11″-14″

A typical scene along a stream or lake shore is almost sure to include the solitary Belted Kingfisher, perched on a overhanging limb or hovering in mid-air, ready to plunge into the water for a fish. The bird looks comical with its oversized bill and huge head topped with a ragged crest. The nest, concealing 7 to 10 white eggs, is at the end of a deep tunnel dug into an earth bank. The Kingfisher flies along the water with a peculiar flight, sometimes fast, sometimes slow, and at brief intervals utters a rattling call. The species ranges widely over the continent, often remaining in northern latitudes as long as there is open water.

COMMON FLICKER *Colaptes aurátus* 13″-14″

The Flicker, our largest common woodpecker, is our only brown-backed member of the family. Frequently called the Yellow-hammer, its identification markings include yellow under wings and tail, "polka dot" breast, black breast band, and a distinct white rump. The male sports a black "mustache" marking on the side of the face. The undulating flight, "wick-wick-wick-wick" call, and "flicka-flicka" note complete its identification. The Flicker is a ground-feeding "ant-eater," but it also includes other insects, wild fruits and weed seeds in its diet. The nest is a deep cavity excavated in a rotted tree, in which five to nine white eggs are laid. Although a few Flickers remain all winter, most of them migrate farther southward.

RED-HEADED WOODPECKER
Melanerpes erythrocephalus 8″-9″

Most colorful of its clan, the Red-headed Woodpecker is the only eastern woodpecker with an entirely red head. In flight, great patches of white are evident. The Red-head not only gleans wood-boring insects from trees, but darts after winged insects in flycatcher fashion. Nuts are an important part of the diet, the Red-head often stores beechnuts and acorns under loose bark and in other small cavities. The nest, excavated in a cavity in a tree or post, contains 4 to 6 white eggs. Red-headed Woodpeckers migrate far and wide, some remaining in the north if food is abundant. The call is a coarse "tcher! tcher!" somewhat like the song of the tree frog.

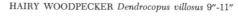

HAIRY WOODPECKER *Dendrocopus villosus* 9″-11″

Of our two white-backed woodpeckers, the larger and less frequently seen is the Hairy Woodpecker, nearly Robin-sized but with a short tail. It is almost identical to its smaller counterpart, the Downy Woodpecker, the chief distinguishing feature besides size being its disproportionately larger bill. In both species the male sports a bright red patch on the back of the head. The Hairy Woodpecker is truly a conservationist of the forest, searching incessantly for insects which destroy leaves, bark and wood. The sharp call of "Peek!" is a welcome sound in dreary winter woods. The nest, an excavated tree cavity lined with a few wood chips, contains 3 to 5 shining white eggs.

27

DOWNY WOODPECKER *Dendrocopus pubescens* 6″-7″

Watch and you will see this friendly little woodpecker as it lights low on a tree and works upward in a jerky fashion, probing into every crevice in search of insects and cocoons. It is at home in open woodlands, orchards, and in shade trees, and has not retreated with the cutting of the forests, as have so many of our woodpeckers. In its black and white garb, the Downy is almost identical to its larger relative, the Hairy Woodpecker. However the latter has a disproportionately larger bill. The Downy excavates its nest hollow in a tree and lays four to six white eggs. A year-round resident, it is a frequent visitor to winter feeding stations.

EASTERN KINGBIRD *Tyrannus tyrannus* 8″-9″

This courageous bird has earned the name "Kingbird" by its fearlessness in defending its nest from intruders. Even the crow and hawks are not immune to its savage attacks. Darting at the molester's back it dives again and again, until the victim has been driven far away. Identification is unmistakable. The bird is all black except the white underparts, the concealed orange crown-patch, and the distinctive white tail band. Kingbirds live and nest in the open country. The nest of weed stalks and grass, lined with plant fibers and rootlets, may be found near the end of a branch, on fence posts, under bridges or on barn rafters. Four to 5 white eggs, brown spotted, are laid. The food is more than 90 per cent insects. Kingbirds winter in tropical America.

GREAT CRESTED FLYCATCHER *Myiarchus crinitus* 8″-9″

The Crested Flycatcher, a true forest dweller, is the most distinctively marked member of his clan. The yellow belly, rufous-brown tail, and slightly crested head make his identification easy. Even in leafy cover this bird announces his tree-top presence with a loud and frequently called "Wheeeep!" One of the unexplained peculiarities of nature is the Crested Flycatcher's habit of including a snake skin in the nest, which is in a cavity in a tree. Here the male pugnaciously sets up guard against any would-be intruder. The nest contains 4 to 6 creamy white eggs, streaked with brown. A voracious eater of winged insects, this beautiful summer resident migrates to the Gulf and Central America.

EASTERN PHOEBE *Sayornis phoebe* 6″-7″

Hardiest of the flycatchers, and one almost certain to turn up in the blustery cold of March, is the Eastern Phoebe. This common gray-brown bird with a black bill can hardly be called "plain," for it has a very distinguishing habit of sitting on a wire or branch near the nest site jerking its tail up and down incessantly. The nest, a neat structure of mud with mossy covering, lined with plant fibers, is built on a solid foundation — a barn rafter, bridge beam, even on a nest shelf — and almost always near water. To further assure identification, the Phoebe repeatedly utters its name in husky unwhistled notes. Flying insects are its chief source of food.

EASTERN WOOD PEWEE *Contopus virens* 6″-7″

Not until the leaves have almost attained full size does the Wood Pewee return from its winter range in Central and South America. We can be certain of its return when we hear the sad, plaintive "Pee-a-wee" song drifting through the woodlands. It is an olive-brown bird with whitish underparts, two distinct wing-bars, and a yellow lower mandible. The cup-like lichen-covered nest, saddled on a horizontal limb at a fork, contains two to four creamy-white eggs speckled with brown. In typical flycatcher fashion, it darts out after passing insects from its tree-limb perch. Insects constitute nearly 100 per cent of the Wood Pewee's diet, making it a highly valuable species.

HORNED LARK *Eremophila alpestris* 7″-8″

The Horned Lark is a bird of the open country, frequenting fields, golf courses and shores. It returns late in the winter from its wintering grounds in the southern states. One of the first birds to nest, it is not unusual to find a female sitting on her clutch of 3 to 5 speckled eggs completely surrounded by snow. The nest is an excavated depression in the ground, lined with grasses. The dark collar and blackish tail of the Horned Lark are distinctive. Tiny feather "horns" can be seen at close range. Horned Larks are seen along roadsides and in fields throughout the summer, gathering weed seeds and insects, or dust-bathing.

TREE SWALLOW *Iridoprocne bicolor* 5″-6″

The Tree Swallow is the first of the swallow family to arrive in the spring, migrating leisurely from its winter home in southern United States. It can readily be identified by its white underparts and dark blue-green upperparts. Tree Swallows normally nest in hollows of rotting trees and old woodpecker holes, but will readily accept man-made nest boxes. Four to seven pure white eggs are laid. Unlike many species, Tree Swallows will nest in close proximity to each other. The female does all of the nest-building and incubating, but both parents feed and care for the young. The Tree Swallow is very beneficial, its food being largely insects.

BANK SWALLOW *Riparia riparia* 5″-6″

The Bank Swallow is the smallest and one of the commonest of the swallows. Brown-backed and clear breasted, it is distinguished from the similar Rough-winged Swallow by the distinct dark throat band. It is a colonial bird, dozens and even hundreds of pairs nesting adjacent to each other in excavations in river banks, railroad cuts and sand diggings. The 4 to 6 white eggs are placed at the end of the cavity, two or three feet from the entrance. Hundreds of these graceful swallows may be seen skimming together over water or fields, catching flying insects. In early fall Bank Swallows gather in large flocks on telephone wires before migrating to South America.

BARN SWALLOW *Hirundo rustica* 6"-8"

The graceful Barn Swallow earns its name rightly, for its feather-lined nest of mud pellets mixed with straw and horse hair is found plastered to the rafters and under the eaves of barns throughout its summer range. Wintering from Mexico to Brazil, the Barn Swallow arrives in Michigan in April. The deeply forked tail, blue-black back and buffy underparts make the bird easily recognized. It is extremely useful, living entirely upon flying insects. Although it is a gentle bird, it will fearlessly attack whatever approaches too close to its nest. The song of the Barn Swallow is a delicate and musical "kvik-kvik!"

PURPLE MARTIN *Progne subis* 8"-9"

The Purple Martin is the largest of our swallows, and is the only one which is blue-black both above and below. The female has dusky-white underparts. It is said that the Indians, before the time of the white man, hung gourds on poles to encourage Martin nesting. Today the favorite nesting sites are the man-made colonial houses to be found throughout the country, although holes in cliffs and cavities in trees are often used. Four to 5 white eggs are laid. The Purple Martin is extremely valuable, consuming huge quantities of flies, mosquitoes, and other flying insects. Its only song is a pleasant liquid gurgling sound. Martins migrate to Brazil.

BLUE JAY *Cyanocitta cristata* 11"-12"

The Blue Jay, a year around resident, is considered one of our most beautiful birds with its plumage of white, blue, gray and black. It is noisy and mischievous, sometimes stealing eggs and young from other birds' nests. On the credit side it is a natural forester, hiding many nuts and seeds which eventually become trees and bushes. It also eats many injurious insects. The Jay is a good mimic, particularly of the Red-tailed and Red-shouldered Hawks. Four to 5 olive-buff eggs, speckled brown, are placed in its nest of twigs lined with rootlets and grasses. Dense pine thickets are preferred as nesting sites. It is a frequent visitor at feeding stations.

COMMON CROW *Corvus brachyrhynchos* 17"-21"

The crow is too well known to require description; his somber black figure and "Caw! Caw!" call are known to almost everyone. Despite open seasons, bounties, and organized crow shoots by hunting clubs, the wily Crow maintains its numbers and continues to pester farmers with its appetite for corn and other grains. The crow's diet also includes insects, mice, and weed seeds, all of which are on the credit side. The nest of sticks, often lined with grape bark and animal hair, is usually placed high in a tree. Three to five pale greenish or pale bluish eggs are laid. With few natural enemies, the nesting is usually highly successful. Crows are resident throughout their range.

BLACK-CAPPED CHICKADEE *Parus atricapillus* 4"-5"

The Chickadee is one of the hardy group of year-around residents. It is very friendly to man, accepting his feeding station handouts in winter and sometimes using his nest boxes in summer. It performs many amusing acrobatics as it goes about hunting under bark scales for insects and their eggs, of which it destroys thousands each winter. The Chickadee is distinctive with its grayish back, black cap and bib, and white cheeks and underparts. The nest hole is usually in a hollow tree, where five to nine white eggs are placed. The Chickadee says its name, "Chick-a-dee-dee-dee," and also whistles a clear "Fee-bee-bee" call, the first note higher than the others.

TUFTED TITMOUSE *Parus' bicolor* 6"-7"

One of the brightest sounds of the winter or early spring woods is the clear whistled "Peter! Peter!" of the Tufted Titmouse. This busy little acrobat, often found in association with its relative, the Black-capped Chickadee, always announces his presence. If the song is not sufficiently distinctive the bird itself is, for no other small gray bird wears a tufted crest. Rusty flanks and a clear breast further aid identification. The nest, in a woodpecker hole or natural cavity, is lined with fibrous bark, hair and leaves. Five to 8 creamy white eggs, marked with brown, are laid. Wild fruits, nuts and insects make up the diet. The Titmouse is not considered to be migratory.

WHITE-BREASTED NUTHATCH *Sitta carolinensis* 5"-6"

The White-breasted Nuthatch is found both summer and winter in our latitude. It is noted for its ability to run head first down a tree trunk, searching for a meal of insects or their eggs, and has thus been nicknamed "the upside-down bird." If you listen you may hear its nasal "Ank-ank-ank" note. Its blue-gray back, black cap, and white face and underparts make identification easy. The nest is in a hollow tree, stump, or man-made box, and contains five to eight white eggs, speckled with brown. In winter the White-breasted Nuthatch is a regular feeding station customer, cracking seeds by wedging them into a crevice and striking them with its bill.

BROWN CREEPER *Certhia familiaris* 5"-6"

The Brown Creeper is a well named bird, for it is seldom seen doing anything but creeping up the trunks of trees. Alighting at the tree base, the Brown Creeper hitches his way, somewhat spirally, up the trunk, searching meticulously in bark crevices for insects, larvae and eggs. Soon he loops inconspicuously to the base of another tree and repeats his "nearsighted" searching. The stiff tail, which serves as a prop, and the down-curved bill are special equipment aiding in the Brown Creeper's work as well as in our identification of him. The nest, hidden behind a loose strip of bark or in a cavity, contains 5 to 8 white eggs, speckled with brown.

HOUSE WREN *Troglodytes aedon 4"-5"*

The House Wren is a fine example of industry and nervous energy. Brown-backed and lacking any distinct facial markings, it is nevertheless easily recognized by the pert and saucy manner in which it holds its tail: straight up, or even tilted forward. It is bold for its size, making dashing attacks on all intruders to its nesting area. The nest of twigs, grasses and feathers may be found in a tin can, old hat, the hollow of a tree or, very commonly, in a man-made house. Here six to eight white eggs, speckled with brown, are laid. This bird is very valuable, its diet being almost all insects. House Wrens winter in the south Atlantic and Gulf states.

GRAY CATBIRD *Dumetella carolinensis 8"-9"*

Busy, saucy, noisy, belligerent — these describe the manner of the trim little Catbird, the smaller of our two common members of the Mockingbird family. Although named and well-known for its petulant catlike mewing, this slate-gray bird sings a very interesting song composed of a jumbled succession of notes and phrases. In quality it resembles that of the Brown Thrasher, our other "Mocker," but does not repeat its phrases as the Thrasher does. Often living close to man, in orchards, shrubs and thickets bordering gardens and fence rows, the Catbird still remains wary and evasive. The well-concealed nest is fashioned of twigs, grape bark, and leaves lined with fine rootlets. Three to 5 greenish eggs are laid.

BROWN THRASHER *Toxostoma rufum 10"-12"*

In form, the Brown Thrasher is very much like the Mockingbird, but its rufous-red underparts and heavily spotted breast make it easy to recognize. The beginner might confuse it with a thrush, but the long tail and curved bill should correct this error. It frequents thickets in open woodlands and brushy hedgerows, as well as shrubbery around houses. Here the bulky nest of coarse twigs, leaves and grape bark, lined with coarse rootlets, is built, either low in vegetation or on the ground. Three to six grayish-white eggs, heavily spotted with brown, are laid. The song is in short phrases, like the Catbird's, only each phrase is repeated. Brown Thrashers winter in the southern states.

ROBIN *Turdus migratorius 8"-10"*

No bird species is better known or more loved by children everywhere than the Robin. The State Bird of Michigan as well as several other states, this widely-distributed thrush amply deserves its "place in the sun." Returning north even before winter's grip has been broken, the Robin seems to symbolize the universal longing for spring. The cheery song as well as its close association with our homes, lawns and gardens further endear the Robin to us. The nest, of mud covered with grasses, rootlets, leaves and strings, is lined with finer grasses. Three to 5 greenish blue eggs are laid. Although a few individuals stay all winter, most Robins migrate to the warm Southland.

WOOD THRUSH *Hylocichla mustelina* 8″-9″

The Wood Thrush is an inhabitant of cool woodlands. Somewhat smaller than the Robin, it is recognized by the reddish-brown back, much redder head, and heavily spotted sides and breast. The rich flute-like song may be heard from early dawn until twilight. Like the other thrushes, it obtains most of its food from the ground eating many insects and some wild fruits. The nest is a cup-like structure of grass, leaves and twigs, strengthened with muck or leaf mold, much like the Robin's nest. It is usually placed in a crotch or on a horizontal limb of a sapling, and contains three to five blue-green eggs. Wood Thrushes winter from Florida southward.

HERMIT THRUSH *Catharus guttata* 7″-8″

The clear sweet flute-like song of the Hermit Thrush wafted on an early morning breeze from the cool secluded woodlands of northern coniferous regions, is one of Nature's most inspiring sounds. Each phrase is a short series of ascending notes, the phrases being pitched in various keys. A closer look may reveal the bird itself, with the Thrush's typical spotted breast, but distinguished from the Wood Thrush and others by the reddish tail. When alarmed, the bird raises and lowers its tail, a further aid to identification. The nest hidden on the ground is built of mosses and coarse grasses lined with pine needles. Three or 4 greenish blue eggs are laid.

EASTERN BLUEBIRD *Sialia sialis* 6″-7″

The Bluebird, a true harbinger of spring, is loved by everyone. The rufous breast and rich blue back of the male make it easy to identify. Although not one of the great singers, its velvety song is rich and pleasing. The diet, consisting chiefly of insects, makes it a valuable bird. Three to 5 pale blue eggs are laid in the cavity of a tree, fence post, or woodpecker hole, but it also readily nests in man-made boxes near our homes. Sometimes there are two broods in a season. Like the young of other thrushes, baby Bluebirds have speckled breasts. During October Bluebirds may be seen in flocks as they start their journey southward.

GOLDEN-CROWNED KINGLET *Regulus satrapa* 3″-4″

Tiniest of our cold-weather birds, the dainty Golden-crowned Kinglet is often found in the company of Chickadees and Nuthatches. Although the bird wears a conspicuous crown — orange in the male, yellow in the female — it usually forages so high in tree tops that the colorful markings go unseen. Keen ears, however, will detect the bird's cheery presence by the high, thin notes it utters as it gleans scale insects and insect eggs from tree branches. In summer the diet changes to small flying insects. The diminutive female produces king-sized families of 8 to 10 creamy eggs, speckled with brown. The nest, of mosses, lichens and bark, lined with rootlets and feathers, is in a coniferous tree.

33

CEDAR WAXWING *Bombycilla cedrorum* 7″-8″

It would be difficult to describe properly the grace and elegance of this lovely bird. Its silky-textured plumage gives it a smooth suave appearance. Outstanding features are its yellow-tipped tail, waxy red wing tips, and pointed crest, the latter seeming to express its every emotion. The manner of flight is distinctive, for as it flies in close formation with others of a flock, it will wheel, then suddenly plunge swiftly downward to a feeding tree. It is very fond of small ripe fruits, but also eats many injurious insects. The nest of plant fibers lined with plant down contains 3 to 5 bluish-white speckled eggs. It is built in a tree or high shrub, and closely resembles the Kingbird's nest.

LOGGERHEAD SHRIKE *Lanius ludovicianus* 9″-10″

The large headed, slim tailed migrant Shrike, with gray above, white below, and wearing a black mask, is a familiar sight in open country of farmlands. Perching on a telephone wire, tree top or some other vantage point, the Shrike scans the vicinity for possible food. If he sights a grasshopper, large beetle or some such tasty morsel, this keen-eyed bird strikes swiftly, then returns to devour his catch or impale it for a future meal. Sometimes small snakes, frogs, mice and birds are also on the menu. The nest, a cup of twigs, stems and grasses is lined with rootlets, plant down, wool or feathers, and is well hidden in a thick shrub.

STARLING *Sturnus vulgaris* 7″-8″

Like the House Sparrow, the Starling was introduced into this country. In 1890 about 100 birds were liberated in New York, and since then their numbers have grown to millions. In spring it is a blackish, iridescent bird with a short tail and yellow bill. In winter the feathers are heavily speckled and the bill is dark. Starlings are year-around residents. The untidy nest of grasses and feathers is built in woodpecker holes, hollow trees, fence posts or nesting boxes, often depriving native species of their homes. Five to 7 pale blue eggs are laid. The Starling's flight is rapid and direct. Food consists of insects, weed seeds, grains and fruits.

RED-EYED VIREO *Vireo olivaceus* 6″-7″

The Red-eyed Vireo, our most abundant vireo, is at home in the forest as well as in the trees of cities and towns. Its monotonous three-noted phrase, repeated from morning to evening, has earned it the nickname of "Preacher Bird." The black-bordered white line over the eye is distinctive, as are the olive-green back and white underparts. The red eye color is difficult to see in the field. The Red-eyed Vireo is a diligent and tireless worker, constantly searching the undersides of leaves for insects. Its basket-like nest, fastened to a horizontal crotch or fork, is made of fibers, birch bark, paper, lichens and bits of hornet nests, bound with spider silk. Its nest is often parasitized by the Cowbird.

34

BLACK-AND-WHITE WARBLER *Mniotilta varia* 5"-6"

Among the earliest arrivals in spring is the dapper little Black-and-White Warbler, often called the "Black and White Creeper." This nickname is well earned, as the bird creeps and climbs up and around tree trunks and limbs, closely scanning the bark for tiny insects. The only black and white striped warbler with which it might be confused, the Black-poll Warbler, has a solid black cap. The thin high-pitched song, "weesee, weesee, weesee, weesee," helps to locate the bird in its woodland haunts. The nest is on the ground, usually at the foot of a tree, and is made of grasses, leaves and mosses, lined with finer materials. Four to 5 white, speckled eggs are laid.

YELLOW WARBLER *Dendroica petechia* 5"

Probably no warbler is better known than the Yellow Warbler, for this little all-yellow songster nests throughout the state, in low easily observed locations. In willow thickets near streams, in bushes along field edges, even in shrubs around homes, the Yellow Warbler builds its dainty but firm cuplike nest of light colored plant bark fibers lined with plant down. Often parasitized by the Cowbird, the Yellow Warbler solves the problem by placing additional nest material over the Cowbird's eggs, thus preventing them from developing. Her own 4 or 5 bluish-white eggs, thinly marked with brown, are then laid. Yellow Warblers are useful as well as beautiful, their diet being almost entirely insectivorous.

YELLOW-RUMPED WARBLER *Dendroica coronata* 5"-6"

With its flash markings of yellow on the crown, rump, and in front of each wing, the Yellow-rumped Warbler is an easily recognized species. It is often considered the most abundant northern warbler, and in migration seems to occur everywhere. Breeding in mixed deciduous and coniferous woods, from northern United States north to the tree limit, the Yellow-rumped Warbler nests in conifers usually at a height of 10 or 15 feet. The nest, a rather bulky affair of plant fibers and grasses, contains 4 or 5 white eggs, speckled with brown. Yellow-rumped Warblers eat insects, seeds and berries, particularly those of the red cedar, bayberry, wax myrtle and poison ivy. They are frequently found here in winter.

OVENBIRD *Seiurus aurocapillus* 5"-6"

The olive-brown back and striped breast give the Oven-bird the appearance of a small thrush, but actually it is a large warbler. It is a common resident of thick moist woodlands, and its ringing call of "Teacher! Teacher! Teacher!" fills the woods from early May well into the summer. It is truly a ground bird, running about in search of such foods as insects, spiders, snails, berries and seeds. It builds a unique nest on the ground, which somewhat resembles an old-fashioned dooryard oven, with the opening at one side. Four to six white eggs, spotted with brown, are laid. Ovenbirds spend the winter from southern United States south to the tropics.

COMMON YELLOWTHROAT *Geothlypis trichas* 4"-5"

This little warbler, sometimes called the Northern Yellowthroat, prefers dense vegetation bordering swamps and watercourses. It hops nervously about in low bushes, well hidden from view, singing its loud clear song which is often described as "Wichity-wichity-wichity!" The male is distinctive with his black mask, olive back and yellow chest. The female is plainer, lacking the mask. The bulky nest, located on or near the ground, is built of bark, leaves, and grasses. Three to five white eggs, brown speckled, are laid. The Yellowthroat is highly valuable with its diet of caterpillars, plant lice, and other injurious insects. The bird winters in the south Atlantic and Gulf states.

AMERICAN REDSTART *Setophaga ruticilla* 4"-5"

The Redstart is one of the most active of the warblers, flitting about with spread tail and wings. Its pleasing five-phrased song resembles "Tsee-tsee-tsee-tsee-tsee!" Redstarts are very easy to identify. The male wears a black garb with bright orange patches on wings and tail, and a white belly. The female is olive-brown above, with yellow wing and tail markings and white underparts. Since Redstarts are so abundant, their diet of insects makes them important economically. The neat nest of plant fibers lined with finely shredded bark is placed in a tree crotch and contains four to five whitish eggs, speckled with brown. Redstarts winter in the West Indies and Central and South America.

HOUSE SPARROW *Passer domesticus* 5"-6"

The best known of the "Sparrows" is neither a sparrow nor a native of our land! The House Sparrow, actually a member of the Weaver Finch family, was first brought to this country from England in 1850 and liberated in Brooklyn. For the next 25 years many additional importations were made, and from these relatively few alien birds has come our vast and widespread House Sparrow population. Although it is a rather handsome bird with its brown coat and black bib, its noisy, messy, pugnacious hordes have made it a generally unpopular species, unprotected and unwanted. The bulky nest, of almost any material placed in almost any location, contains 4 to 7 white eggs, marked with olive.

BOBOLINK *Dolichonyx oryzivorus* 7"-8"

The Bobolink is a happy-go-lucky bird that seems to wear its suit upside down, since the male is black below and cream above. The female is pale buff with dark stripings on the underparts. In early and mid summer Bobolinks may be found in meadows and pastures of the north. There they build their nests of grasses and weed stems on the ground or on clumps of grass; 4 to 7 grayish-white eggs, splotched with brown, are laid. Their song is a cheerful bubbly, tinkling medley of notes. In late summer, en route to their wintering grounds in South America, they become the drab, unpopular "rice birds" or "Reed birds" of our southern states.

EASTERN MEADOWLARK *Sturnella magna* 9"-11"

The Meadowlark a bird of the open fields, returns from its winter range in southern United States in early spring. Some individuals remain here through the winter. The yellow breast crossed with a black V and the white outer tail feathers make identification unmistakable. The clear variable whistle-like song can be heard throughout the day. The Meadowlark is not a true lark, but instead belongs to the blackbird family. Its nest is on the ground, a dome-like structure of grasses, open on one side. Here 4 to 6 white eggs, speckled with red-brown, are laid. The Meadowlark is very beneficial, its diet being almost entirely insects.

RED-WINGED BLACKBIRD *Agelaius phoeniceus* 8"-10"

No marsh is complete without the Red-winged Blackbirds, which return to the northern states very early in the spring. The first flocks to arrive consist entirely of males, the females following soon after. The male is an all-black bird with red shoulder epaulets bordered with yellow, while the female is dressed in modest brown, somewhat streaked with ashy white. Also, she is smaller than the male. The nest is usually found near water in reeds, cattails or low bushes, or in hayfields, and contains three to five brown-streaked white eggs. The song of the Redwing may be interpreted as "Kong-quer-ree!" or "O-ka-lee!" Food consists of insects and weed seeds.

NORTHERN ORIOLE *Icterus galbula* 7"-8"

In his gay coat of fiery orange and black, there is little hint of the Northern Oriole's close relationship to the Cowbird, Grackle, and other members of the blackbird clan. Returning from his Central American wintering grounds in May, when trees are in leaf and insects abundant, the Oriole immediately announces his arrival with his rich piping notes. The nest, a baglike structure hung high in a shade tree, usually near the limb end, is composed of swamp milkweed, bark fibres and strings, lined with horsehair or grasses. One of nature's most monotonous sounds is the incessant crying of the young Orioles, a characteristic which has earned for them the name of "crybabies of the woods."

COMMON GRACKLE *Quiscalus quiscula* 11"-13"

The big iridescent Grackle, easily identified by its long wedge-shaped tail and light colored eye, is one of the first migrants to return in the spring. The smaller female is duller in color. It is a trim bird, and seems to strut as it walks about on the ground in search of food. Grain, weed seeds, fruits and many insects make up its diet. Normally a bird of the marshes and forest-bordered lakes and streams, now it often takes up residence close to man's dwellings. Conifers and cattail marshes are favorite nesting sites. The bulky nest of grasses and muck contains 3 to 7 bluish-white eggs, speckled with brown. Grackles winter in southern United States.

BROWN-HEADED COWBIRD *Molothrus ater* 7″-8″

The Cowbird is one of the smallest of the blackbird family, and the male is the only "blackbird" with a brownish head. The female is brownish gray. Cowbirds have earned their name because of their association with cattle, where they will be found around their feet and on their backs. Cowbirds parasitize other birds' nests with their own speckled eggs, leaving them for the foster parent to incubate and raise. Because the young Cowbirds grow so fast and require so much food, the young of the parasitized species (usually fly-catchers, warblers, vireos and sparrows), often starve to death. The song is like a squeaky gate, often uttered in flight. Cow-birds winter in southern United States.

SCARLET TANAGER *Piranga olivacea* 7″-8″

The male Scarlet Tanager, with his red body and black wings and tail, is unmistakable. He is most often seen and recognized when migrating north from South America in the spring. His secretive summer haunts are deep shady wood-lands, where he is often heard but seldom seen singing his nasal, robin-like song. The loose nest of twigs and weeds, lined with finer materials, is placed near the end of a hori-zontal limb and contains three or four bluish-white eggs, speckled with brown. In fall the male's red becomes olive-green, more closely resembling the year-around plumage of the female. Their food consists mostly of insects.

CARDINAL *Cardinalis cardinalis* 8″-9″

The Cardinal, one of winter's cheeriest sights, is our only red bird with a crest. Formerly a southern bird, in recent years the Cardinal has established permanent residence in the northern states. The nest which is placed in low bushes or vines, often close to houses, consists of medium twigs, leaves or paper, and grape bark, lined with finer twigs. Three or 4 bluish-white eggs, speckled with brown, are laid. The male is very attentive, singing to his duller-colored mate and feeding her as she incubates the eggs. There are many vari-ations to the Cardinal's shrill whistle, two common ones being "What-cheer! What-cheer! What-cheer!" and "Whoit-whoit-whoit-whoit-whoit!" Diet includes wild fruits, seeds and many insects.

ROSE-BREASTED GROSBEAK
Pheuticus ludovicianus 7″-9″

The Rose-breasted Grosbeak resides chiefly in second-growth woodlands, orchards, and thickets near streams. Dis-tinctively colored in black and white, with its triangular breast patch of rose-red, the male is unmistakable. The female is brown with a striped head, but her thick powerful bill helps to identify her. The Rose-breast is a valuable insect eater, consuming large quantities of tent caterpillars, canker worms and potato beetles. The nest, usually located in low trees or bushes, is made of twigs and grasses lined with fine rootlets. Four or 5 pale blue eggs, splotched with brown, are laid; the male helps with the incubation. The song is Robin-like in quality, and the call is a sharp metallic "ick!"

INDIGO BUNTING *Passerina cyanea* 5"-6"

The male and female Indigo Bunting appear quite different, the male wearing brilliant indigo blue garb while his mate is dressed in plain brown. Arriving in May from Cuba or Central America, they are often seen perched on roadside trees and bushes. The male sings his oft-repeated ditty, resembling "Sweet, sweet-zoot, zoot-suet, suet!", from a perch high on a tree. The nest of leaves and grasses is usually placed low in the crotch of a sapling or shrub. Four to 5 pale bluish-white eggs are laid. Indigos eat insects, weed seeds and wild fruits. In fall the males assume the dull garb of the females.

EVENING GROSBEAK *Hesperiphona vespertina* 8"-9"

An infrequent but very welcome migrant to our southern Michigan feeding stations and box elder thickets is the chunky, stout-billed Evening Grosbeak. The bird is a common winter visitor in the northern part of the state. Highly gregarious, these distinctive black, yellow and white birds make their appearance in sizable flocks and are recognizable even at a distance by their undulating flight. Evening Grosbeaks nest in Canada and as far south as northern Michigan, usually building quite high in conifers. The loosely constructed nest of twigs, lined with fine rootlets, contains 3 or 4 blue-green eggs lightly marked with brown. Originally, and quite mistakenly, the bird was thought to sing only at evening. Hence the name.

AMERICAN GOLDFINCH *Spinus tristis* 5"-6"

The Goldfinch is unmistakable in its dress of yellow with black wings, tail and cap. Frequently called the "Wild Canary," its main diet consists of weed seeds, grain and wild fruit, although some insects are eaten. The bounding, undulating flight and cheerful "Per-chee-she-she!" song give an impression of constant exuberance. Goldfinches build late in summer and place the nest of plant bark fibers, lined with thistle or cattail down, in crotches or forks of trees. Three to six bluish-white eggs are laid. When winter comes the male becomes dull olive-yellow, like the summer female. Goldfinches remain all winter, frequently visiting at feeding stations.

RUFOUS-SIDED TOWHEE *Pipilo erythrophthalmus* 8"-9"

The Red-eyed Towhee is often called the "ground robin," and is an inhabitant of the bushy undergrowth. It is an active noisy bird, scratching among leaves for food. The black head and upperparts, white underparts, and robin-red sides make the male easy to identify. The female wears a similar garb, but with brown replacing the black. The nest is placed on the ground or low shrubs, and is made of dead leaves and bark, lined with grasses. Four to five white eggs, speckled with brown, are laid. Insects, wild fruits and weed seeds are eaten. The "Drink-your-teee!" song and "Che-wink" call of the towhee are distinctive. The bird winters in southern United States.

VESPER SPARROW *Pooecetes gramineus 6"-7"*

As the Vesper Sparrow sits on a fence post or bush at the edge of a field it may look, from a distance, like any one of several field-dwelling Sparrows. But let it flit off to another perch, and instantly it identifies itself by the distinctive white outer tail feathers. The only other bird of summer pastures and weedy fields with such marking is the Meadowlark, whose V-shaped yellow breast and larger size are unmistakable. The sweet song of the Vesper is quite like the Song Sparrow's, but simpler and more deliberate. The ground nest of coarse grasses lined with finer grasses, rootlets and hairs, contains 4 or 5 greenish-white eggs, speckled and scrawled with brown.

DARK-EYED JUNCO Junco hyemalis 6"-7"

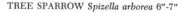

When the chill of early winter fills the air we may look for the little Dark-eyed Juncos to descend from the north in considerable flocks. Throughout the long winter they are common, searching the fields and edges for weed seeds, visiting well-stocked feeding stations, and cheering us with their simple but musical trill's. Juncos appear rather drab in their suits of dull gray, but the white outer tail feathers, and the white belly contrasting sharply with the slaty breast make identification unmistakable. The breeding range is from northern United States (including northern Michigan) to the tree line. The nest, on the ground, contains 4 or 5 bluish-white eggs, speckled with brown.

TREE SPARROW *Spizella arborea 6"-7"*

When the frosts of autumn come, driving less hardy birds south, flocks of Tree Sparrows begin drifting down from the north. Here, in snow covered and wind blown weedy fields and borders of woodlands, the "Winter Chippy" spends the season, adding welcome cheer with its merry tinkling notes. Although it may come to feeding stations for a handout of small grain, the Tree Sparrow needs no such help, finding ample food in the weedstalks of the field and pasture edges. The single spot on the clear breast and the reddish cap serve to positively identify this winter resident. When winter fades into balmy spring the Tree Sparrows are suddenly gone, seeking their far northern breeding grounds.

CHIPPING SPARROW *Spizella passerina 5"*

The Chipping Sparrow is the most unassuming of all the sparrows. It is very trusting, and often builds its nest in vines or shrubbery close to our door. The nest of grasses, lined with horsehair or fine rootlets, contains four or five bluish-green eggs, with brownish markings. The Chipping Sparrow is a trim little creature, with brown-streaked back, clear breast, black line through the eye and white line over the eye. The bright rufous cap is a good field mark. The song is a series of rapidly repeated chips, all on one pitch. Chipping Sparrows are very useful, eating many harmful insects besides weed seeds and a few small grains. They winter in the southern states.

FIELD SPARROW *Spizella pusilla* 5"-6"

More a resident of bushy pastures than the open field, the little Field Sparrow perches on a fence post or small bush and utters his sweet, pensive song. The song, much more distinctive than the plain little songster, is an oft-repeated series of notes beginning slowly but speeding up to a hurried trill. The Field Sparrow is identified by its combination of reddish cap, clear grayish breast, and a pinkish bill. The nest, usually on the ground or in a grassy clump or low bush, is made of coarse grasses lined with finer grasses or hair. About 4 pale green eggs, spotted with reddish brown, are laid. A common summer resident here, the Field Sparrow winters to the Gulf Coast.

WHITE-THROATED SPARROW

Zonotrichia albicollis 6"-7"

In migration or on the northern nesting grounds, the White-throated Sparrow announces its presence with its sweet clearly-whistled song. "Old Sam Peabody, Peabody, Peabody!" it seems to say. North of the border it may be interpreted as "Oh sweet Canada, Canada, Canada!" This beautiful sparrow may be identified by its white throat patch, striped black and white crown, and yellow spot before each eye. It may often be heard in the dry woods, scratching in dead leaves or hopping after insects. Breeding in the spruce belt of northern United States and Canada, the White-throat prefers brushy edges and pastures for its nest, which may be on the ground or in low bushes.

SONG SPARROW *Melospiza melodia* 5"-7"

One of nature's cheeriest sounds in late winter or early spring is the melodious, variable song of the Song Sparrow. This familiar brown bird has a streaked breast with a conspicuous spot on its center. The rather long tail is pumped when the bird is in flight. Song Sparrows like roadsides and thickets, but will often feed and nest in close proximity to man. The nest, placed on or near the ground, is made of grasses, lined with finer material. They lay four or five bluish-white eggs, speckled with brown. Food consists of weed seeds and insects. Many Song Sparrows visit our feeding stations in winter, although some migrate southward.

SNOW BUNTING *Plectrophenax nivalis* 6"-7"

One of the delightful winter-time surprises for Michigan motorists is to come upon a flight of almost white "Snow birds," rising in a compact flock from the roadside and wheeling with the precision of a group of shore birds. Like a cloud of windblown snowflakes, the birds drift off to some new feeding grounds, to dine on weed seeds. As spring approaches, these "harbingers of winter" disappear to the north, making their way to the barren Arctic wastes. Here, in summer dress of black and white, the Snow Buntings nest on the ground or in rock crevices, building a nest of plant materials lined with fur and feathers. Four to 5 whitish eggs, spotted with brown, are laid.

41

R S BUTSCH

drawing by Robert S. Butsch

COMMON LOON
42

Special Michigan Birds

by Robert W. Storer

What you consider the special birds of Michigan in part depends on where you come from. Taken as a whole, the birds of our state are eastern, hence visitors from the west may take special pleasure in looking for the more than thirty species of wood warblers which are known to summer in Michigan or in becoming acquainted with birds like the Rose-breasted Grosbeak, Indigo Bunting, Baltimore Oriole, and Scarlet Tanager, which have familiar counterparts west of the Great Plains. On the other hand, visitors from the East Coast can find such western species as Western Meadowlark, Brewer's Blackbird, and Le Conte's and Clay-colored sparrows. The large north-south extent of the state makes possible a wide range of habitats from cold spruce bogs in the north to deciduous forests in the south. Thus the breeding birds include such northern species as the Black-backed Three-toed Woodpecker, Yellow-bellied Flycatcher, Gray Jay, Boreal Chickadee, Palm Warbler, and Evening Grosbeak and such southern forms as Bobwhite, Red-bellied Woodpecker, Prothonotary Warbler, and Louisiana Waterthrush.

The Great Lakes which border the state provide the nearest approach to an oceanic environment and support large numbers of wintering Old-squaws and large breeding populations of Herring and Ring-billed gulls and Common and Caspian terns. Great Black-backed Gulls have moved in from the East Coast and have increased in numbers along the southeastern shores of the state. Other marine or coastal species such as the Purple Sandpiper, phalaropes, jaegers, and Black-legged Kittiwake appear as rarities in the large flights of water birds which stop off on the Great Lakes on their way to and from the breeding grounds in the north.

The extensively wooded Upper Peninsula is one of the best places in the east to see Common Ravens, and Common Loons and Pileated Woodpeckers also occur there in good numbers.

Upland game birds are numerous in suitable habitats. Ruffed Grouse and American Woodcock are widely distributed in the state. Sharp-tailed Grouse are not uncommon in the north, but probably only one dancing ground of the Greater Prairie Chicken remains in the northern part of the Lower Peninsula. Ring-necked Pheasants are common in the southern part of the state, and Wild Turkeys have been reintroduced in several areas of the Lower Peninsula. The elusive Yellow Rail evidently migrates through Michigan in some numbers and has been found nesting in several places in the northern part. Spruce Grouse, which are protected in the state, are found through much of northern Michigan. They are rarely found in the jack-pine plains of the Lower Peninsula but are more numerous in mixed stands of jack-pine and spruce in the Upper Peninsula. For several years, Dr. William L. Robinson of Northern Michigan University has been studying a marked population of Spruce Grouse on the Yellow Dog Plain in northwestern Marquette County.

To many, the most impressive Michigan bird is the Sandhill Crane, and the state is its easternmost stronghold. The two major breeding areas in Michigan center around Schoolcraft and Luce counties in the Upper Peninsula and Calhoun, Jackson, and Livingston counties in the southern part of the Lower Peninsula. Censuses of the latter area in 1952, 1953, and 1954 yielded fall counts of from 173 to 197 birds, and the population of the Upper Peninsula was thought to be even larger. Since then, the populations have increased considerably, aided by the conservation efforts of the Michigan Audubon Society and Dr. Lawrence H. Walkinshaw, biographer of the species (*The Sandhill Crane*, Cranbrook Institute of Science, 1948) and an energetic and enthusiastic authority on all cranes.

Good places to watch Sandhill Cranes in the Upper Peninsula are around the Seney National Wildlife Refuge in Schoolcraft County and near Sleeper Lake north of Newberry in Luce County. In the Lower Peninsula, two of the best areas are on the Bernard W. Baker Sanctuary north of Marshall in Calhoun County and on the Phyllis Haehnle Memorial Sanctuary between Ann Arbor and Jackson, in Jackson County.

The cranes arrive on the marshes of southern Michigan from late February through March. The nests, consisting of large mounds of vegetation are most often found in the remote parts of large marshes. The clutch consists of two (rarely one) eggs, which are laid in April or early May. Incubation requires 32 days and the young first fly at the age of three months. In late summer and early fall, family groups can often be seen foraging in open fields; in October these groups join others in preparation for the southward migration in November. Freshly molted adult cranes in the fall are gray, but by the time they return to the breeding grounds, they are literally rusty. This is not the result of molt but of the birds' frequent preening with the bill, to which dirt containing iron compounds has become attached.

Although the official State Bird is the widespread and familiar Robin, there is a bird, the Kirtland's Warbler, which is not known to nest outside of Michigan. In fact, its breeding range is limited to parts of the northern third of the Lower Peninsula.

Kirtland's Warbler was originally described from a specimen taken May 13, 1851, near Cleveland and named for the Ohio naturalist, Dr. Jared P. Kirtland. In 1879, its wintering grounds in the Bahamas were discovered, but the mystery of its breeding grounds was not solved until 1903. In that year, Norman A. Wood, curator of birds at the University of Michigan Museum of Zoology, found the first nest of the species in western Oscoda County. Wood returned to the breeding grounds many times to study the warblers, and his successor, Dr. Josselyn Van Tyne, made a long-term, detailed study of the bird's life history until his untimely death in 1957. The Ohio ornithologist, Harold F. Mayfield, another long-time student of the species, is the author of a book (*The Kirtland's Warbler*,

Cranbrook Institute of Science, 1960), which is fascinating reading and won for its author the coveted Brewster Medal of the American Ornithologists' Union.

Kirtland's Warblers nest on the ground in stands of young jack-pines and hence are also known as Jack-pine Warblers. The principal requirement appears to be pine-branch thickets near the ground. The females spend most of the time in these thickets and both parents move through such thickets on their way to and from the nest. Under natural conditions, suitable stands of jack-pines come up after fires. Such stands are usually colonized when the pines are approximately six feet tall and are deserted by the time they reach a height of twenty feet. Stands of less than eighty acres are rarely used.

As improved fire-fighting techniques decreased the areas burned, the potential breeding grounds of the Kirtland's Warbler shrank. Consequently, in 1958, the Michigan Department of Conservation, in cooperation with the Michigan Audubon Society, set aside three tracts of state forest amounting to eleven square miles to be managed for the Kirtland's Warbler. This landmark in the conservation of a non-game bird was augmented five years later when the United States Forest Service dedicated a 4010-acre tract in the Huron National Forest for a similar purpose. Between May 1 and August 15, permits are required for visitors to these areas. There is no charge, and permits for areas managed by the state can be obtained at the Mio office of the Michigan Department of Natural Resources and for the area in the Huron National Forest at the United States Forest Service office at Mio.

Male Kirtland's Warblers can be readily found by their loud, emphatic song, which on calm days can be heard for a quarter of a mile or more. They are also less wary than most birds and usually can be approached quite closely so that their tail-wagging and other field marks can be easily observed.

Their loud, persistent singing has been used in four censuses of the species. The first, in 1951, yielded a count of 432 males, and the second, in 1961, 502 males. By 1971 the count dropped to the dangerously low figure of 201 males. There is considerable evidence that parasitism by Brown-headed Cowbirds is a potent factor in lowering breeding success in these warblers. Research spearheaded by Professor Nicholas L. Cuthbert of Central Michigan University has led to a program of control of cowbirds, largely through trapping. Presumably as a result of cowbird control in 1971, no appreciable decrease in the warblers was noted in the 1972 census. More extensive control in 1972 led to an encouraging increase in fledging success. The close cooperation of Federal and State agencies, conservation groups at all levels, and informed and interested individuals has been particularly gratifying. We urge that visitors to the nesting grounds of this rare species refrain from disturbing the birds, and especially their nests. Sets of photographs have been prepared and duplicated for sale in the area. Please do not attempt to photograph the bird while the population is at a dangerously low level. — *Museum of Zoology, University of Michigan, Ann Arbor*

photo by Karl Maslowski

BARN OWL

Where To Find Birds In Michigan

by Clarence J. Messner

Few of us can travel widely in search of birds except at vacation time. This is why experienced birders make it a point to learn their local area well. Fair habitat close to home can yield more pleasure and more birds than excellent habitat too distant for frequent visits. Most of us, however, enjoy new places and the opportunity to see new birds. Our state offers great and attractive variety both for the person who wants to search far afield and for the stay-at-home.

Michigan, nearly 60,000 square miles in area, 400 miles from north to south and 300 miles from east to west, contains many diverse habitats for wildlife. Surrounded by the magnificent Great Lakes, this state is an extremely fruitful birding area. Possessing rich farmlands and remnants of the original prairie in the south, cut-over forest land in the central and northern portions, and regrettably few remnants of the primitive virgin forest, Michigan has an abundant bird fauna. Birding areas in this state may be placed conveniently in such categories as: parks and recreation areas, river valleys and shore lines, peninsulas, and sanctuaries and experimental stations. Space here permits only a brief discussion of some interesting areas. Pettingill's *Guide to Bird Finding East of the Mississippi,* 1951, Oxford University Press, New York, gives detailed directions to many of the places mentioned below. His article in "Audubon Magazine" for May-June, 1958, is also very useful for locating good birding spots in northern Michigan.

For persons living in or near the metropolitan area of Detroit, there are the lands known as the Southeastern Michigan Recreation Areas and the Huron-Clinton Parkway System. Productive areas for birding are: Bald Mountain Area near Lake Orion, Pontiac Lake Area about five miles west of Pontiac, Highland Area near the village of Highland, Kensington Park near Brighton, Lower Huron Metropolitan Park near Romulus, Stoney Creek Park near Rochester, and Waterloo Area northeast of Jackson. Descriptive folders for these and other areas may be obtained from the Michigan Department of Conservation in Lansing and from the Huron-Clinton Metropolitan Authority in Detroit.

Most of the major state parks satisfy the conditions of terrain, cover, food, and water that attract birds and other wildlife. The largest and most diversified are: Hayes State Park a few miles southeast of Jackson, Warren Dunes State Park near St. Joseph, Muskegon State Park at Muskegon, Ludington State Park six miles north of Ludington, Hoeft State Park near Rogers City, Hartwick Pines State Park northeast of Grayling, Wilderness State Park west of Mackinaw City, Tahquamenon Falls State Park near Newberry, and the Porcupine Mountains State Park in the far western end of the Upper Peninsula. Michigan also has one national park, Isle Royale National Park, far out in Lake Superior.

River valleys and lake shores make excellent birding areas for a number of reasons. They produce good food and cover, a variety of habitats, and are often natural migration routes. Impoundments on rivers usually have good marshes which attract wildfowl. The St. Clair-Detroit River system is one of the best in the state for waterbirds, which can be found all along its course through most of the year. The 3000 miles of Great Lakes beaches provide excellent habitats for birds. With their long stretches of sandy and rocky shores, bordered by beach pools, stands of shrubby vegetation, and forests, they are attractive to many species, both land and water birds, and especially to shorebirds, gulls, terns, ducks, and grebes. The Saginaw Bay area is a particularly good example of lakeshore habitats, and directions for finding birds here were published by Kenaga in "The Jack-Pine Warbler," for June, 1956. Michelson's Landing on the headwaters of the Muskegon River west of Houghton Lake is a place where nesting waterbirds can be seen easily. Some attractions here are Ospreys, Great Blue Herons, Florida Gallinules, Least Bitterns, and, nearby, Greater Prairie Chickens and Sharp-tailed Grouse.

Points of land jutting out into the Great Lakes are nearly always good for birding during spring and fall migration. Fish Point and Tawas Point in Saginaw Bay, Waugoshance Point in Wilderness Park, the tip of Leelanau Peninsula north of Traverse City, North Cape east of Erie in Lake Erie, and the two famous points in Lake Superior, Whitefish Point in the east and Keweenaw Point in the west, are all excellent for migrating birds. Usually these points are as good for land birds as for waterbirds.

In Schoolcraft County near Germfask is the Seney National Wildlife Refuge, primarily for waterfowl, but with breeding populations of Sandhill Cranes, Yellow Rails, LeConte's Sparrows, and other interesting species. North of Seney, where M-77 crosses the Schoolcraft-Alger county line is De Rosia's Rustic Cabins, center of an area that has been fantastically productive in recent years of nesting northern species. Here, and along the equally good Adam's Trail just northwest of De Rosia's, have been found nests of Yellow-bellied Flycatchers, Olive-sided Flycatchers, Palm Warblers, Lincoln's Sparrows, Boreal or Brown-capped Chickadees, and other northern specialties. Near Battle Creek is the Kellogg Bird Sanctuary, a gift of the Kellogg Foundation to Michigan State University. Of an increasing number of wildlife areas administered by the state, two are particularly good, the Rose Lake Experimental Station near Lansing and the Swan Creek Experimental Station near Allegan. Most of Michigan's 40-50 Game Areas are usually good for waterfowl and general birding. A listing of Game Areas may be secured from the Department of Natural Resources. The Michigan Audubon Society is itself the owner of several sanctuaries, all excellent places to bird and all described elsewhere in this booklet.

As we enjoy the wildlife and wild country of Michigan, so must we accept responsibility to protect and preserve it for all time.

— *1572 Jones Drive, Ann Arbor, Michigan.*

Field Study Helps

by Homer D. Roberts

The beginning study of birds in the field requires a minimum of equipment. One should have: (a) a good pair of binoculars (7 x 35 is considered ideal for all around use); (b) A pocket-size field guide, preferably with color illustrations (Peterson's *A Field Guide to the Birds* is standard for this part of the country); (c) a small notebook for special notes, nest locations and data, etc.; and (d) a daily check-list for easy recording and filing of each trip's list of species (The Michigan Audubon Society's daily check-lists are excellent for Michigan-area field trips). A metal tape for taking measurements of nest heights and sizes is also very useful. More exacting studies will require the use of measuring calipers and small scales for measuring growth rates and weights of unfledged young.

When a bird is spotted there are definite characteristics to look for, including comparative size, color, distinctive or peculiar habits, details of bill, feet and tail, and song or call.

Three common species of birds are frequently used as standards of size. In referring to comparative sizes we may say that a bird is (e) "a little larger than an English Sparrow," (f) "about as big as a Robin," or (g) "a little smaller than a Crow."

Some birds have bold color patterns which make them quite easy to recognize. The black and red colors of the Scarlet Tanager (h) and the solid blue of the Indigo Bunting (i) are unmistakable. Other birds have flash markings which, although not large, may stand out and greatly aid identification. The Marsh Hawk (j) bears a prominent white rump patch, while the Cedar Waxwing (k) has an easily-spotted yellow tail-band.

A bird may reveal its identity by some simple yet distinctive habit. The Phoebe (l) twitches its tail nervously as it sits on a branch or wire near the nest site, while the Spotted Sandpiper (m) "teeters" as it walks along the shore. Flight characteristics may help in identifying certain species. The Goldfinch (n) has a bounding, undalating flight pattern, while the Great Blue Heron (o) flaps laboriously and steadily on an even course.

The habitats in which birds are found are often clues to their identity, or at least they help to narrow the field of possibilities. Many species are narrowly restricted to specific locations or types of habitat, and are rarely found elsewhere during the breeding season. Grebes, bitterns and herons spend most of their lives in marshes or at the edges of reed or cattail-lined ponds. The open meadow is the surest place to locate a Bobolink, Meadowlink, Field or Vesper Sparrow. Bushy growth along woodland edges is the home of the Indigo Bunting, the Song Sparrow, and many others. The jackpine plains of central Michigan is the only place to seek the Kirtland Warbler. And the forest is the home of the Ovenbird, the Red-eyed Vireo, and various kinds of woodpeckers. Such limitations in habitats, as well as the food obtainable there, have resulted in physical adaptations most easily observed in the feet and bills. Closely seen, these adaptations may constitute excellent points of identification.

Interesting examples of specialized bills include: the long, probing bill of the Woodcock (p); the flat, sieve-edged straining bill of ducks (q); the strong strong flesh-tearing bills of birds of prey (r); and the heavy, seed-crushing bills of Cardinals and other finches (s).

Examples of specialized feet include: the climbing feet of the woodpeckers (t); the lobed feet of marsh-dwelling Coots (u); the grasping talons of owls (v); and the webbed swimming feet of the Loon (w).

Many species have distinctive, easily recognized tails. Among these are: the short spined tail of the Chimney Swift (x); the deeply forked tail of the Barn Swallow (y); and the long narrow tail of the Brown Thrasher (z).

When leaves cover the trees in late spring and throughout the summer, many birds are much less frequently seen than heard. Thus a knowledge of their songs is important in locating and identifying them. When an unfamiliar song or call is heard, track it down to its source. Then, having positively identified the bird by size, color, and other field marks, make an association between its song and some easily-remembered phrase. The Red-eyed Towhee, for example, seems to say "Drink your tee-ee-e-e!" The Cardinal's fast-phrased and shrill "Whee-whee-whee-whee-whee!" is quite like a man whistling for his dog. Some birds, like the Killdeer, Phoebe, Bobwhite and Whip-poor-will say their names. Good references for sound identification can be found in the article "Michigan Bird Publications" on pages 77-78.

How To Study Birds

by George J. Wallace

There are many ways of gleaning useful information out of observations on birds, in addition to merely watching them for enjoyment. Study projects are almost limitless. Some can be carried out with a minimum of equipment; others require more sophisticated and complicated gadgetry. The investigator will have to use his own judgment as to how involved he wants to get.

Obvious essentials are a bird glass or binocular (we recommend 6 x 30's, 7 x 35's or 8 x 40's, all available from MAS) for accurate identification and for close-up behavior or life history studies. For waterfowl addicts a spotting scope or telescope is very useful. A small pocket notebook, or paper mounted on a clipboard, can be used for recording data, then these can be transferred to more permanent notebooks at home. For nesting studies a pair of calipers and a ruler for measuring the growth of young birds and scales or balances for taking weights are useful. Some ingenious investigators have rigged up electrical wiring devices at nest boxes for recording trips by the parents to the nest. Many people now use tape recorders for recording songs and calls; once recorded the songs can be used for playbacks to call birds in for closer observations. Perhaps the ultimate in studying birds in the field is the use of radio transmitters which emit signals when attached to birds so that their daily movements or portions of a migration can be followed. Some of these more advanced techniques are beyond the means, or ambitions, of many people. The references listed at the end of this article explain these methods of study more fully.

Some of the traditional types of studies, that can be carried out with or without complicated gadgetry, are described below.

1. Life Histories. Many new facts can still be learned about the nesting habits of our common birds. Select a conveniently available species that interests you and watch it through the nesting season — its time of arrival, if it is a migratory bird; its daily round of activities; and the role of the sexes in nest building, incubation and care of the young.

2. Migration studies. Many observers in Michigan submit detailed records to the Michigan Bird Survey. We need, of course, well authenicated records of rare birds, and records of common birds at unusual times and in unexpected places, but we also need such simple data as last dates for transients in the spring and departure dates for birds in the fall. Too many people just record first dates. Or you may want to specialize on hawk flights, warbler waves, or shorebird movements. Such observations are needed to determine the status of each species and to learn the year to year fluctuations in populations.

3. Banding. You may wish to band birds in conjunction with the above studies, or merely want to band birds to learn what you can about

them. In general, banding large numbers of spring and fall transients is unrewarding; rarely will you ever hear of one of them again. But if you concentrate on summer or winter residents, they may return again and again and stay with you throughout the summer or winter seasons. (See Nickell's article on bird banding in this bulletin.)

4. Endangered Species. There is much concern now about certain birds whose continued survival is threatened by our destruction or misuse of their environment. The Department of Interior (Fish and Wildlife Service) has issued a list of 36 species (or subspecies) of birds believed to be in imminent danger in the United States; on a world-wide basis the number of endangered species and subspecies is believed to be about 318. Many others not in immediate danger are threatened by our advanced technology and despoilation of habitats. The September, 1969 *Jack-Pine Warbler* gives a list of endangered and declining species of Michigan birds. Keep records on the status of these birds, if opportunity affords.

5. Predatory Birds. Hawks and owls are in a special category of endangered species because they come at the end of complicated food chains and suffer most when any link in the chain is affected. But there are unanswered questions concerning the status of these birds. Why, for instance, are the Red-shouldered Hawk and Marsh Hawk declining, while the Red-tailed Hawk, and perhaps the Sparrow Hawk, seem to be increasing? Why are Barred Owls disappearing in southern Michigan, while the Great Horned Owl continues to thrive?

6. Pesticides and Birds. Chemical tests (analyses) are too costly and technical for the layman to undertake, but field observations on decline, mortality, nesting success, and other information following spraying operations are badly needed.

7. Feeding Stations. Many people feed birds but few make critical observations on food preferences, seed selection, social behavior and dominance relations. Can you work out any effective techniques for discouraging "nuisance" birds at feeders and attracting the more desirable kinds?

These are only a few of the studies that you can undertake in hopes of furthering scientific knowledge and of enriching your own lives by engaging in a wholesome pastime.

SOME REFERENCES FOR THE STUDY OF BIRDS
(Some available from the MAS Bookshop)

Berger, A. J. How to Make a Life History Study. *Enjoying Birds in Michigan* (2nd edition). Michigan Audubon Society.

Hickey, J. J. 1953. *A Guide to Bird Watching.* Garden City, New York. A classic for beginning bird watchers. Reprinted several times.

Odum, E. P. 1943. Techniques in Life History Study. *Jack-Pine Warbler,* 21:39-47.

Reichert, Robert J. and Elsa Reichert. 1951. *Know Your Binoculars.* A 12-page leaflet explaining use and care of binoculars. Distributed free with purchases or available for 10¢ from Mirakel Optical Co., Mt. Vernon, New York.

Wallace, G. J. 1963. *An Introduction to Ornithology.* Macmillan. Chapter 16, on Ornithological Methods, explains methods of study, in field and lab, in considerable detail.

— Department of Zoology, Michigan State University, East Lansing, Michigan.

Bird Banding

by Walter P. Nickell

One of the most significant developments in the study of bird migration within the last fifty years has been the use of numbered aluminum bands on the legs of individual birds. Before that time most means of marking birds for later identification were more or less haphazard and disorganized.

No two band numbers are ever duplicated, so that identifying a bird on its later capture is as positive as fingerprinting in the identification of human beings. The most productive results of banding are obtained when birds are banded in their nesting areas and in their winter quarters. It has been known for perhaps 100 years that most birds nesting in any given area have a strong tendency to return to the same area each year as long as they live. This is called homing. Within the last fifty years, researchers have discovered that a considerable number of birds go back to their same winter quarters just as they return to their familiar nesting grounds in the spring. A Michigan man, Dr. Josselyn Van Tyne, late Curator of Birds at the Museum of Zoology at the University of Michigan, was probably the first investigator to prove this point. In 1931 he banded 99 Indigo Buntings in the Peten District of Guatemala. Six of these buntings were recaptured at the same place in 1932.

Returns are obtained when birds return to the original place of breeding, whether it is the nesting area or the wintering area. *Recoveries* are obtained when someone captures the bird or finds it dead at a locality other than the place of banding.

Some remarkable recoveries have been made on birds, in some cases as far as 12,000 miles from the point of banding. The most consistent long range returns from birds banded in Michigan have been from as far away as Labrador to the north and Chile to the south. Of birds banded in Michigan, the longest range recoveries have been made on Herring Gulls, Ring-billed Gulls, Common Terns and Black-crowned Night Herons. All of these are fairly large birds which may be found around seashores and streams so that they are more easily located than the smaller songbirds which, on dying, are often hidden by vegetation. It is a good habit, when a bird is found dead, to examine its legs for bands.

One of the most revolutionary advances in the techniques of capturing birds for banding is the use of nylon mist nets in which the birds become caught when they are flying through thick vegetation. Wire mesh traps are still used by some banders, but most have changed to mist nets during the last ten to fifteen years.

Bird banding is licensed by the United States Fish and Wildlife Service at the Patuxent Research Refuge at Laurel, Maryland. It is illegal to capture birds without a permit. This same agency sends out all the bands which are used in the western hemisphere. Once each year the bander sends in a complete report which is placed on I.B.M. cards, so that when a banded bird is found and the band number is sent in, all of the details as to where banded, by whom, and the date of banding can be obtained for the recoveree within a few minutes.

The extent of bird banding at the last official report for 1967 is indicated by the fact that nearly two and a half million bands were issued in that year to the holders of 1,900 master permits and 1,000 sub-permits. There were 647,133 banding reports and 99,487 recovery reports received at Patuxent that year.

Bird banding is now a massive international effort in which nearly all the major areas of the world are engaged to some extent. By means of various publications of regional, national and international scope, the results of world banding efforts are correlated and published. Thus, banding has become probably the most important single medium of world-wide research on bird distribution, migration, longevity and other important aspects of ornithology.

There are approximately 100 licensed banders in Michigan, mostly concentrated in the southern tier of counties in the state. Most states, including Michigan, have bird banding associations. Regional banding organizations are the Northeastern, Eastern and Inland Bird Banding Associations. Each organization has its own quarterly publication. The publication of the only international banding organization is *The Ring*, published in Wroclaw, Poland.

— *Cranbrook Institute of Science. Bloomfield Hills, Michigan.*
Present address: Route #5, Box 127B, Clinton, Tennessee.

DISTRIBUTION OF RECOVERIES ON COMMON TERNS
Banded by Walter P. Nickell (1953-1968)

The above map shows by black dots the locations of at least 46 recoveries received from common terns banded in southern Michigan from the Bay City area of Lake Huron down the Lake St. Clair-Detroit River waterway to southwestern Lake Erie.

Beginning with the place of banding, these recoveries show a distribution in the following states, provinces, countries and insular areas: Michigan (3), Illinois (1), Ontario (3), Ohio (4), Pennsylvania (1), New York (1), Massachusetts (1), Louisiana (1), Florida (4), Jamaica (2), Guatemala (1), El Salvador (1), Costa Rica (2), Panama (7), Colombia (4), Trinidad (1), Surinam (1), Ecuador (3), Peru (3), Chile (1), and the Azores (1).

Attracting Birds

by Homer D. Roberts

One of the best ways to become acquainted with birds is to attract them to your own garden or lawn. By means of special plantings, summer bird baths, winter feeding stations, and nesting boxes and shelves, the bird population of an area can be increased substantially.

A number of trees and shrubs blend well into a general landscaping plan and serve the further purpose of providing summer nesting sites as well as late fall and winter food supplies for birds. These include red mulberry, black cherry, mountain ash, red cedar, honeysuckle, highbush cranberry, Japanese barberry, silky dogwood, Michigan holly and buckthorne.

Many of the hardy permanent resident and winter visitor birds will become regular and easily-observed visitors to your feeding station, provided a few simple rules are observed:

1. Make your feeder simple, avoiding gadgets and moving parts which might frighten the birds. Leave one or more sides open.

2. Place the feeder in a wind-protected place, yet not so surrounded with close-up bushes as to provide an easy "ambush" spot for cats.

3. Provide a variety of foods, since different species of birds have different food preferences. A well-stocked feeder will include small grains, sunflower seeds, cracked corn, cracked nuts, grit, suet, bread crumbs, crushed dog biscuit, and water.

4. Keep your feeder supplied with food every day, so that birds which come to depend upon your daily hand-outs will not suffer when their needs are greatest.

Some of the common visitors to a well-cared-for feeding station may include the Cardinal, chickadee, Downy Woodpecker, Tufted Titmouse, White-breasted Nuthatch, Blue Jay, junco, Tree Sparrow, goldfinch, English Sparrow and Starling. In outlying regions the Bobwhite and Ring-necked Pheasant may be among your boarders.

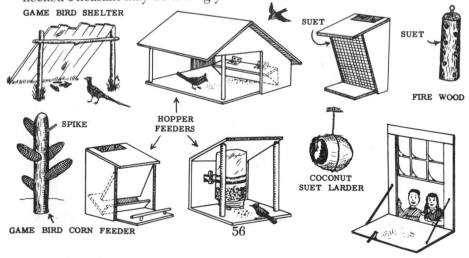

GAME BIRD SHELTER

SUET

SUET

FIRE WOOD

SPIKE

HOPPER FEEDERS

COCONUT SUET LARDER

GAME BIRD CORN FEEDER

56

About fifty species of birds have been known to nest in man-made boxes or shelves in the United States, several of which may easily be attracted to your own yard. The following suggestions will aid in planning, constructing and placing your bird house:

1. Build for a specific species, following the size suggestions in the chart below.

2. Use wood, left in a natural finish or painted a dull neutral color. (The colony house of the purple martin may be white to better reflect the sun's rays.)

3. Provide for clean-out, ventilation and drainage (see picture suggestions below).

4. Leave the interior surfaces of deep-cavity houses rough to aid the young birds in climbing out.

5. Place in the open on a post, along the edge of a garden, orchard or field.

	FLOOR OF CAVITY (INCHES)	DEPTH OF CAVITY (INCHES)	ENTRANCE ABOVE FLOOR (INCHES)	DIAMETER OF HOLE (INCHES)	HEIGHT ABOVE GROUND (FEET)
Wood Duck	10 x 10	16-18	14-16	3½	15-30
House Wren	4 x 4	6-8	2-6	⅞-1¼	6-10
Bluebird	5 x 5	8	6	1½	5-10
Tree Swallow	5 x 5	6	3-5	1½	6-15
Flicker	7 x 7	16-18	14-16	2½	6-20
Chickadee	4 x 4	8-10	6-8	1¼	5-15
Downy Woodpecker	4 x 4	8-10	6-8	1¼	6-20
Red-headed Woodpecker	6 x 6	12-15	9-12	2	12-20
Crested Flycatcher	6 x 6	8-10	6-8	2	8-20
Robins - Phoebes	7 x 7	(Shelf-one or more sides open)			6-15
Screech Owl	9 x 9	12-15	9-12	3¼	10-30
Purple Martin	6 x 6	6	1	2½	15-20
Prothonotary Warbler	3½ x 3½	6	4-4½	1¼	2-10

CLEAN-OUT, VENTILATION AND DRAINAGE SUGGESTIONS

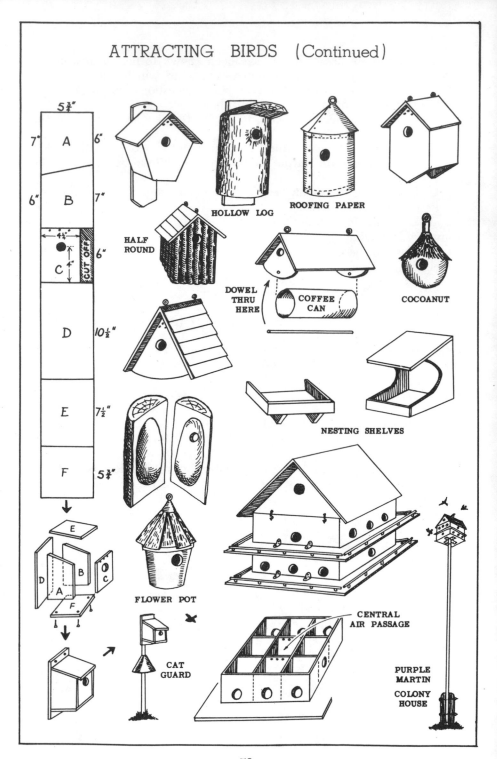

5¾"

7" | A | 6"

6" | B | 7"

4½"

CUT OFF

C | 4" | 6"

D | 10½"

E | 7½"

F | 5¾"

E

D | B | C

A

F

HOLLOW LOG

ROOFING PAPER

HALF ROUND

DOWEL THRU HERE

COFFEE CAN

COCOANUT

NESTING SHELVES

FLOWER POT

CENTRAL AIR PASSAGE

CAT GUARD

PURPLE MARTIN COLONY HOUSE

Some Factors Affecting Bird Populations

by Eugene E. Kenaga

Factors affecting bird populations can arbitrarily be divided into two categories: those caused by man, and those not caused by man. Factors caused by man include purposeful, direct effects such as hunting, fishing, and scientific experiments, and indirect or accidental effects such as those caused by man's changing the environment by drainage, building highways, and clearing land for cultivation or for buildings.

Purposeful population control of birds is subject to state and federal laws relating to their preservation and management. Most species of Michigan birds are protected. "Protected" means that the nest, eggs, young and adult birds may not be molested or taken except within the provisions of the laws. Only three species in the state have no protection from either state or federal law, the House Sparrow, Common Starling and American Crow.

Many species of birds are classed as game birds and may be hunted in accordance with state laws, or state and federal laws in the case of migratory game birds. At present there is a restricted fall open season on these migratory game birds: geese, ducks, rails, Common Gallinule, American Coot, Common Snipe, American Woodcock; and on the following resident game birds: Ring-necked Pheasant, Ruffed Grouse, Greater Prairie Chicken, Bobwhite, and Sharp-tailed Grouse. The open seasons and bag limits for these species are set by the state and, for some, by the federal government.

All other bird species in Michigan are protected throughout the year by federal laws, state laws, or both, except for some special cases. A farmer or landowner may, on land owned or occupied by him, kill hawks (except eagles and ospreys) or owls while they are doing actual damage to poultry or other domestic animals. Birds which are destroying property, such as grain, may be taken only by special permit.

The Michigan Department of Natural Resources and the U. S. Fish and Wildlife Service may, under certain conditions, issue special permits for (a) collecting birds, their nests or eggs for scientific purposes, (b) keeping pets and decoys for non-commercial purposes, (c) importing live birds into the state, (d) propagating wild waterfowl or game birds, or (e) exhibiting birds in public zoological parks. The Michigan Department of Natural Resources can supply details concerning application for such permits.

Violators of laws for the protection of wildlife should be reported to the proper authorities. Mention of such violations to the local conservation officer, even without evidence or prosecution, may lead to prevention of future violations.

Indirect control of birds results mostly from man-caused environmental changes. Man has exerted a profound effect on the natural environment. Many species of birds are very specialized in their requirements for food, shelter, nesting, and courting, having become adapted to special ecological niches over many hundreds of years. Habitat changes often occur gradually, allowing birds to move to new locations, or to adapt to the changes. In recent years, however, man's expanding populations and improved technology have resulted in rapid habitat changes and the complete elimination of large areas of certain types of habitat required by some birds. Despite accidental bird losses due to television towers, picture windows, highway traffic, etc., most bird species would probably maintain their population levels if their breeding habitats were not disturbed or destroyed. Today both the physical and chemical means of changing our environment by man are greatly increased. The bulldozer and the innumerable products of our industries and civilization have produced changes which perhaps match all those of our previous human history. Human sewage, detergents, pesticides, fertilizers and air contaminants are some of the major chemical causes of changes in our environment. Drastic habitat changes are commonplace in our civilization. The changes need not necessarily affect the bird directly. Any widespread interruption in a food chain may be more effective in eliminating a bird population than death from immediate causes.

The natural factors affecting bird populations are climatic change, competition for food, predation and parasites, which birds have experienced throughout the history of their species. Some species have been able to adapt to environmental changes and are increasing in number and range, while others have not been able to adjust to the new conditions and are declining. The numbers of birds in a given time and locality represent a dynamic balance, continually subject to change. In Michigan, during the last 20 years, the Redwing and Common Grackle appear to have increased greatly in numbers. The Western Meadowlark and Brewer's Blackbird are now breeding widely in the state and the Yellow-headed Blackbird has begun to nest in the Saginaw Bay area. These changes among the blackbird family appear to be related to their adaptability to various habitats. As the climate on earth warms, as it has in Michigan in the last 60 to 80 years, some species have advanced northward. Among these are the Cardinal, Tufted Titmouse, Golden-winged Warbler and Mockingbird. Some species such as the Canada Goose and Turkey, well suited to certain Michigan habitats, were thinned or extirpated by hunters before 1900, but have now repopulated many areas of Michigan as a result of restocking and protection from hunting. In spite of heavy parasitism by the Cowbird and shrinking habitat of suitable Jack-Pine areas, the Kirtland's Warbler appears to be maintaining its precarious population level.

In the Saginaw Bay area, the Black-crowned Night Heron, Bald Eagle, American Egret and Screech Owl were seen commonly before 1952. By 1954 these species were rarely seen and were no longer known to nest in the area. The number of individuals of these species dropped off to nearly zero and have remained so. The exact cause of these population declines may never be completely known as they are rarely due to a single factor, but it is well documented that certain persistent fat soluble pesticides are now part of the daily human diet, and this is also true for many species of birds and other organisms. Chemicals such as DDT, dieldrin and some other persistent, chlorinated hydrocarbon insecticides at specified dosage rates in food have been shown to affect the reproduction of certain species of birds. These critical dosages are within the possible contamination levels caused by the use of such pesticides. It is well documented in recent literature that species such as the Bald Eagle, Osprey, Robin, and Herring Gull contain high residues of persistent pesticides.

Although we know a great deal now about the factors involved in the fluctuations of bird populations, we still have much to learn about them. These changes in bird populations are of interest to us not only because of the birds themselves, but even more because they have very important implications for the life of man on earth.

— *3309 Isabella Road, Midland, Michigan.*

photo by Edward M. Brigham II
YOUNG LEAST BITTERNS IN NEST

The Michigan Audubon Society And Its Activities

by H. Lewis Batts, Jr.

At the time the Michigan Audubon Society was incorporated, in 1904, people lived mostly in rural communities and nature was part of their lives — although they may not have understood their real relationships to the living things around them. Since then, sparsely settled rural communities have evolved into densely populated ones, and to people living there "nature" seems remote and less important. They may vaguely understand a relationship to the sun, but their artificial environment of plastic, glass, cement, steel, and aluminum makes it difficult to establish rapport with perishable wild flowers, insects, frogs, and birds, or to see important relationships among living creatures and rocks, soil, air, and water, much less to comprehend modern man's dependence upon such things for his very existence.

The Society's incorporators, only a small group of people mutually sharing an enjoyment of birds, were concerned with simply promoting interest in native birds and in conserving wildlife and other natural beauty in Michigan. These concerns, adequate though they may have been in 1904, now are expanded into an educational program designed to meet the changed needs of today. The purposes of this educational program and of the Society itself, therefore, are:

1) to develop in the people of Michigan a better understanding and appreciation of our natural surroundings and of the problems we face in the management of our natural resources.

2) to provide opportunities for constructive outdoor living through organized programs of study and group activities.

3) to provide a statewide program of leadership training in the field of nature study and conservation.

4) to cooperate with all agencies, organizations, and institutions concerned with conservation, outdoor education, and natural sciences.

5) to maintain sanctuaries and promote wildlife protection programs.

6) to sponsor and participate in ornithological and ecological research.

The Michigan Audubon Society's educational program, devised to accomplish these purposes, emphasizes the education of citizens toward understanding man's role in the interrelatedness of all living things because a well-informed citizen acts wisely when given the opportunity. This educational program takes various forms — depending upon the needs, interests, and talents of the people involved.

Here is a brief outline of the Society's effective program of conservation education for children and adults, for members and the general public.

Activities of Junior Audubon Clubs and Day Camps, and school visits to sanctuaries and nature centers stimulate interest and provide information so that children will become knowledgeable, responsible adults whose attitudes reflect an awareness of their role in the natural world.

Day Camps for children are operated several weeks each summer (since 1957) by MAS chapters.

Nature Counselors Training Camp is conducted in early summer to give intensive training to leaders of summer camp nature programs (YM-YWCA, Boy and Girl Scouts, CYO, private camps) so they may gain practical experience in leading groups in nature activities and so they may learn: techniques for identifying Michigan vegetation, animals, rocks and minerals; how to make collections; nature photography; games and skits; etc.

Campouts, held in the spring and fall since 1938, are enjoyable weekend outings for MAS members to get acquainted with each other and with different natural areas of Michigan through guided hikes, informative campfire programs, and the sharing of outdoor experiences and techniques.

Field trips are scheduled for various parts of the state and are led by people who are well acquainted with the usual natural features of those areas.

Sanctuaries are owned and maintained for the conservation of natural communities and for use in conservation education programs. Nearly 2,000 acres of typical or unique, natural or wild, land and water areas are protected and used in educational programs — places where the curious child or adult has opportunity to learn why and to ask questions. Through direct observations people can better come to understand some of the intricate relationships of the natural world. Sanctuaries are sites for Day Camp and Nature Counselors Training Camp; campouts and field trips; public programs; research by students and serious amateurs working on ecological or other wildlife projects; school class visits; etc.

A library consisting of hundreds of books, journals, magazines, and reprints mostly about birds is maintained at the Society's headquarters for use by members.

A book shop is operated as an educational service to members and to the interested public — providing assistance to those desiring more information about wildlife through books, photographs, drawings, paintings, carvings of natural objects, binoculars, bird feed, bird houses and feeders.

The Munger Fund maintains slides and motion pictures for loan to schools, civic groups, and others.

The Society's publications are vehicles of its education program bringing to members and others results of scientific investigations and news of the Society and its many activities. A bi-monthly newsletter, free to members, contains Society news and chapter activities; schedules of events; comments on pertinent and timely conservation issues. It is influential at state and national levels and plays an active role in making people aware of their environment and what is happening to it.

The Jack-Pine Warbler, the official organ of the Society, makes available to its readers the results of research and other observations by serious amateurs, students, and professionals especially in ornithology (usually life history, population, and distributional studies); miscellaneous articles on conservation topics, wild flowers, insects, amphibians, reptiles, mammals, natural areas; camera studies; etc. Well-written articles and good photographs are always welcomed by the editors; sample copies are available from the Society's headquarters. The Michigan Bird Survey, seasonal research on bird distribution, is initiated by the Society and its results appear in *The Jack-Pine Warbler*. It is published in March, June, September, and December and is sent free to members and in exchange for over 50 national, state, and local publications. Miscellaneous publications such as notices of special activities, field check lists, and *Enjoying Birds in Michigan* are released from time to time.

All of these activities and the people involved in planning and conducting them *are* the Michigan Audubon Society but it has a definite organization. As a corporation, it is designated as non-profit and tax-exempt for income tax purposes. The control of all its activities is in the hands of its approximately 1500 members — who delegate to a Board of Directors the day-to-day operation of the Society.

Each year, usually at the end of January, twelve members of the Board are elected for three-year terms at the annual meeting of the Society. The Board then elects its four officers, appoints standing and ad hoc committees, and recognizes active past presidents of the Society and representatives of its more than 20 chapters as voting members of the Board. All the activities and business of the Society are controlled by the Board acting through about a dozen standing committees and several temporary committees as needed.

Throughout most of its existence, the MAS has been operated only by volunteers and its headquarters were located wherever its officers lived or worked. In 1956-58 the Society had its first paid director, with an office at the Society's Haehnle Sanctuary at Jackson. Since then, its headquarters have been in Kalamazoo, an office being operated at Kalamazoo College (1958-62), then at the Kalamazoo Nature Center since 1962.

A permanent, state headquarters office with a full-time Office Manager attending to Society affairs provides stability and the machinery for action. Lists of members of the Society, of its Board of Directors, committees, and chapters may be obtained from the headquarters office.

The many committees, chapters, officers, etc., are coordinated through this office and the strength of the Society depends primarily upon the effectiveness and efficiency of planning and operations at the committee and chapter levels.

Financial support for everything the Society does comes from membership dues, sales, fees, contributions, and a small endowment — none of which is adequate for the needed programs of the Society. Memberships and contributions through special gifts and bequests are welcomed by the Society to further its effective, many-faceted program.

— *Kalamazoo Nature Center, Kalamazoo, Michigan.*

photo by Bernard Baker

TUFTED TITMOUSE AT FEEDER

Michigan Audubon Society Sanctuaries

by Mabelle Isham

Michigan Audubon Society's first sanctuary was donated to the Society by Bernard W. Baker of Marne in 1941 to provide a refuge for the endangered Sandhill Cranes. It is located in Convis Township of Calhoun County over the heart of the former government swamp land known as the Big Marsh, an important nesting area for the Sandhill Cranes.

In the decade prior to the acquisition of the sanctuary, Bernard W. Baker, Lawrence H. Walkinshaw, and others became concerned over the dwindling crane population which seemed coincident with the increased drainage of Michigan marshes, the choice nesting sites of the cranes. Because of these men who pioneered interest in sanctuary land, the cranes have restored their population, and other sanctuaries have been given to the Society.

The Bernard W. Baker Sanctuary has grown from the original gift of 491 acres to 897 acres by means of an 85-acre addition from members in 1943 and 1960, a gift of 110 acres from the Kresge Foundation in 1965, and a 200-acre adjoining farm with buildings, purchased by the Society through a loan in 1965. This farm will provide the site for an environmental center when funds become available.

In 1948 a small lodge was constructed by volunteers, directed by Harold Wing. During 1962 it was enlarged with two bunk rooms and indoor washroom facilities to meet state health requirements for conservation education camps.

A self-interpreting trail, the Iva E. Doty Native Flower Trail of short loops and total length of one and one-half miles, is separately endowed and maintained. It begins at the trail's interpretative shelter near the Lodge, and wends southerly through many differing habitats. Iva E. Doty, a former resident of Battle Creek, has assured future generations an opportunity to learn about Michigan's southern wildflowers here.

The Society's second sanctuary is the Voorhees Brothers Wildlife Sanctuary, located in Lee Township, Calhoun County. This was given to the Society by Mrs. Charles Voorhees in 1948 and provides a fine example of a natural, unpastured woodlot of beech-maple associates over its 40 acres, especially a delightful profusion of spring flowers. There are no buildings.

In 1949 Miss Jennie Putnam donated to the Society its third sanctuary, the Riverbank Sanctuary, near Manistique. It is located in Schoolcraft County on the beautiful Indian River. There are 23 acres of spruce-hemlock associates which provides the Society with a diversified flora and fauna. Some of the area schools use this sanctuary for biological studies. There are no facilities.

67

In 1955, Casper Haehnle of Jackson donated to the Society 497 acres, the major part of the Mud Lake Marsh located in Henrietta and Leoni Townships of Jackson County, as a memorial to his daughter, Phyllis. The sanctuary bears the name, the Phyllis Haehnle Memorial Sanctuary.

Many groups and individuals enjoy the study opportunities in the differing habitats, especially the water birds and Sandhill Cranes. Upland was added when friends and members purchased an adjoining 160 acres in 1961 so that a total of 657 acres of "green island" is preserved in Jackson County for the future. There are no buildings.

Mr. and Mrs. William A. Vawter of St. Joseph presented the Society with its fifth, the Lew Sarrett Sanctuary in memory of the local poet during the summer of 1964. It is located in Hagar and Benton Townships of Berrien County, and provides a variety of biota on its 170 acres along the Paw Paw River. This sanctuary assures a haven for wildlife in an area of expanding urban development. A wildlife pond was excavated in 1967. A naturalist-director opened the new interpretive center to the public in May 1970. Ponds, trails and boardwalks, with teaching stations have been added.

The first Michigan Audubon Society Nature Center, Seven Ponds, was licensed to the Society by Mr. and Mrs. H. Ripley Schemm of Grosse Pointe Farms in 1966. It is located in Dryden Township of Lapeer County, and provides bog-lakes, uplands, fields, and woods. The donors financed a building from which the educational activities are conducted. In May 1972 Mr. Paul Townsend of Metamora donated 70 additional woodland acres to provide a total of 243 acres.

A seventh sanctuary, the Martha Mott Preserve, was presented to the Society during the 1971 fall campout by Mr. Charles Mott and Mr. and Mrs. David BeshGetoor of Kalamazoo. The 80-acre tract consists of a sand blow and varied habitats traversed by a small stream. It is located in Almena Township of Van Buren County, northwest of Kalamazoo city. The Audubon Society of Kalamazoo has stewardship over these enticing prairie, marsh and wildlife acres.

Michigan Audubon Society's seven sanctuaries have been preserved for this and future generations by the generosity of those with foresight and recognition of the needs of people and wildlife. Many members and friends have sacrificed to assure these lands for all. The maximum use for wildlife and people will mean continual guard, wise management, and supporting funds through the years. The Society has enjoyed a fine spirit of cooperation with the Michigan Department of Natural Resources for the benefit of the people and wildlife of Michigan.

More details and future plans for the development of the individual sanctuaries may be obtained from the Society's headquarters. The maps which accompany this article will help you to find your nearest sanctuary. You'll enjoy visiting all to find that each offers something unique and cherishable.

— *Shagbark Trails, Rt. 1, Bellevue, Michigan.*

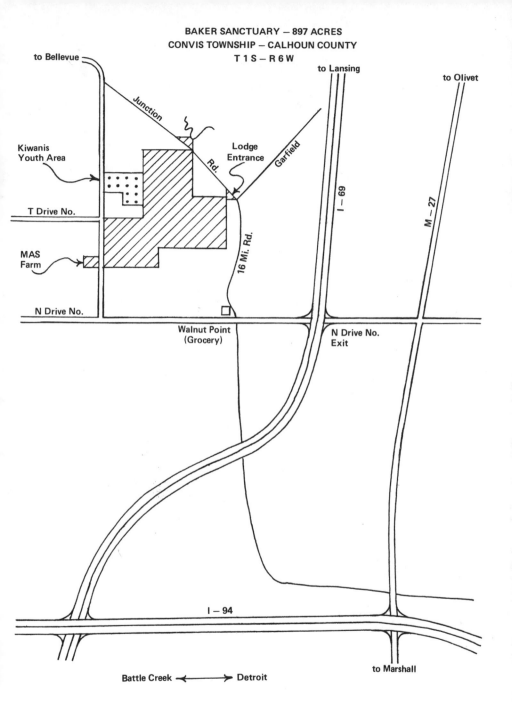

BAKER SANCTUARY — 897 ACRES
CONVIS TOWNSHIP — CALHOUN COUNTY
T 1 S — R 6 W

to Bellevue

to Lansing

to Olivet

Junction

Kiwanis
Youth Area

Lodge
Entrance

Garfield

Rd.

I — 69

M — 27

T Drive No.

16 Mi. Rd.

MAS
Farm

N Drive No.

Walnut Point
(Grocery)

N Drive No.
Exit

I — 94

Battle Creek ← → Detroit

to Marshall

HAEHNLE SANCTUARY — 687 ACRES
LEONI TOWNSHIP — JACKSON COUNTY
T 2 S — R 1 E

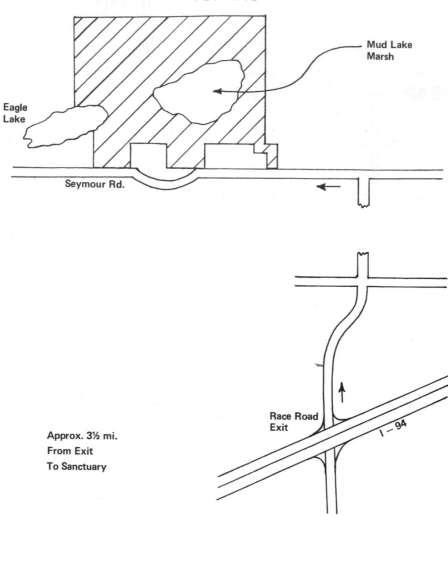

Mud Lake Marsh

Eagle Lake

Seymour Rd.

Race Road Exit

I – 94

Approx. 3½ mi.
From Exit
To Sanctuary

Jackson ⟵⟶ Detroit

RIVERBANK SANCTUARY – 23 ACRES
HIAWATHA TOWNSHIP – SCHOOLCRAFT COUNTY
T 42 N – R 16 W

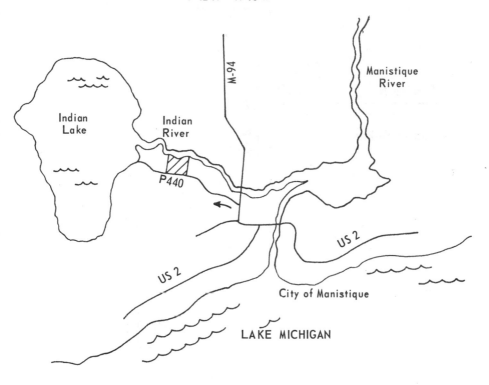

VOORHEES SANCTUARY – 40 ACRES
LEE TOWNSHIP – CALHOUN COUNTY
T 1 S – R 5 W

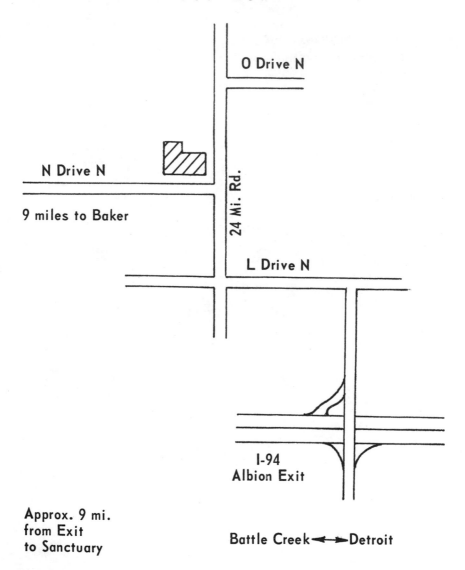

O Drive N

N Drive N

9 miles to Baker

24 Mi. Rd.

L Drive N

I-94
Albion Exit

Approx. 9 mi.
from Exit
to Sanctuary

Battle Creek ◄──► Detroit

LEW SARETT SANCTUARY — 135 ACRES
HAGAR TOWNSHIP — BERRIEN COUNTY
T3S—R18W

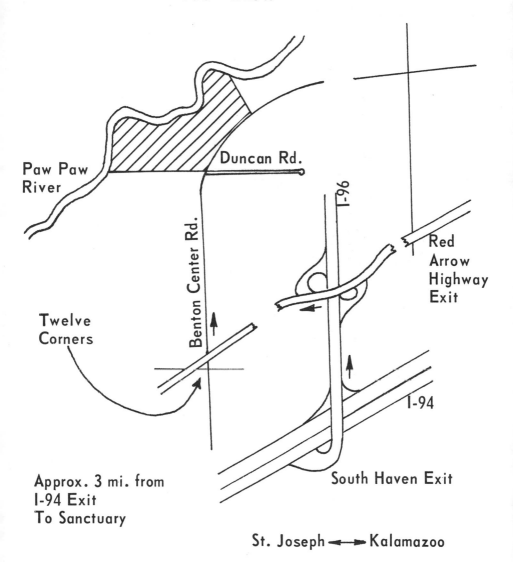

SEVEN PONDS NATURE CENTER — 243 ACRES
DRYDEN TOWNSHIP — LAPEER COUNTY
T6N-R11E

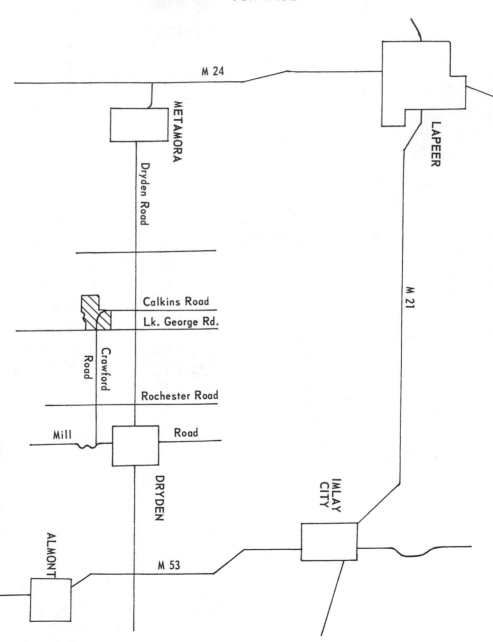

MARTHA MOTT PRESERVE — 80 ACRES
ALMENA TOWNSHIP — VAN BUREN COUNTY
T 2 S — R 13 W

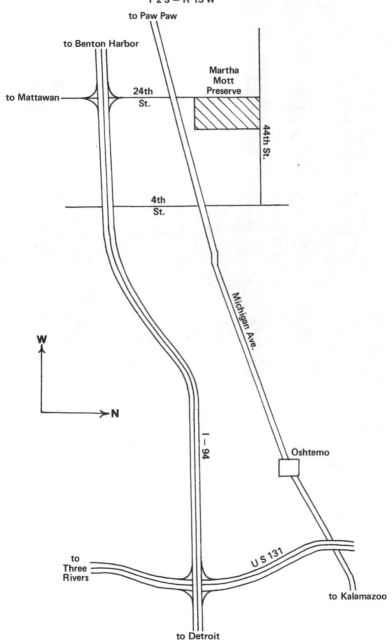

to Paw Paw

to Benton Harbor

Martha Mott Preserve

to Mattawan

24th St.

44th St.

4th St.

Michigan Ave.

W

N

I — 94

Oshtemo

to Three Rivers

U S 131

to Kalamazoo

to Detroit

PINE GROSBEAKS

76

drawing by Robert S. Butsch

Michigan Bird Publications

by Harold D. Mahan

To assist you in your enjoyment of Michigan's birds the following publications which cover Michigan species will be useful. Although several are now out-of-print, most of the more recent publications can be obtained from your Michigan Audubon Society Bookshop.

Field Guides. These are pocket size, well illustrated publications that are essential for identifying birds in the field. All contain plates showing similar species. Most are printed with waterproof covers.

A Field Guide to the Birds. Eastern Land and Water Birds, by Roger Tory Peterson. 1947. Houghton Mifflin Co., Boston. 290 pp. 1000 illustrations, 500 in full color. (For many years this has been the bird-watcher's "bible." Differences in similar species are indicated with small lines. Text contains much useful information on field marks and voice, confusing species, and range of each species. Appendix sections include "Accidentals" and "Subspecies." This publication is now printed in a less expensive, soft cover edition. Index tabs for quick identification also are available.)

Audubon Field Guide. Small Land Birds of Eastern and Central North America from Southern Texas to Central Greenland, by Richard H. Pough. 1949. Doubleday and Co., Inc., Garden City, N.Y. 312 pp. Over 400 full page color illustrations of 275 species. (Like Peterson's *Field Guide*, similar species are arranged on the same plate. All color photos are grouped together in the center of the book, which some birders consider convenient. In addition to information on identification, habits, voice, and range, the text also includes a description of nests and eggs which is helpful.)

Audubon Water Bird Guide, by Richard H. Pough. 1956. Doubleday and Co., Inc., Garden City, N.Y. 352 pp. 623 illustrations of 258 species; 485 in full color. (A companion guide to the above, written in a similar style, but covering those species frequenting aquatic habitats.)

Birds of North America, by Chandler S. Robbins, Bertel Bruun, and Herbert S. Zim. 1966. Golden Press, Inc., N.Y. 340 pp. Over 1500 full color illustrations. (There are several unique features about this very compact book: it covers all of North America, it includes detailed distribution maps of each species, it also shows sonagrams — visual reproductions of bird songs — for the majority of species illustrated. Other features include identification marks including song descriptions for most species and, for a few groups, such as warblers and sparrows, colored plates showing the whole spectrum of variations within the group. Available in hard and less expensive soft cover editions.)

Keys. Unlike field guides, these publications are for more difficult to identify specimens while in the hand. The descriptions are much more detailed. Although many keys have been published, two are particularly useful for Michigan birders:

A Manual for the Identification of the Birds of Minnesota and Neighboring States, by Thomas S. Roberts. 1949. The University of Minnesota Press, Minneapolis. 738 pp. (For the more serious birder and bird bander, the keys, descriptions, and summaries of bird groups in this publication are very helpful. Details of plumages for the majority of species are excellent.)

Birds' Nests, by Richard Headstrom. 1949. Ives Washburn, Inc., N.Y. 128 pp. and 60 black and white photographs. (A very handy book for those interested in identifying bird nests.)

Regional Michigan Bird Books. These publications contain information about limited Michigan areas. In general, arrival and departure dates, abundance, and nesting of the species in the area covered are presented in these publications:

The Birds of Isabella County, Michigan, by Nicholas L. Cuthbert. 1962. Edwards Bros., Ann Arbor. 204 pp. (Along with a description of this central Michigan area and its avifauna, this publication also presents the status of each species throughout the state.)

Birds of the Detroit-Windsor Area, A Ten Year Survey, by Alice H. Kelley, Douglas S. Middleton, Walter P. Nickell, and the Detroit Audubon Society Bird Survey Committee. 1963. Bull. 45, Cranbrook Institute of Science, Bloomfield Hills. 119 pp. (Covering four southeastern Michigan counties and three adjacent Ontario counties between 1945-55, this is one of the most carefully documented of state bird publications. A supplementary volume, *Changes in the Bird-Life of the Detroit-Windsor Area, 1955-1965,* by Alice H. Kelley, published by Cranbrook in 1966, adds to the original list. Also, *A Field List of Birds of the Detroit-Windsor Region,* by Ralph A. O'Reilly, Jr., Neil T. Kelley, and Alice H. Kelley, published in 1960, by Cranbrook, is an abbreviated guide to the original publication.

State-Wide Michigan Bird Publications. These publications treat our avifauna on a state-wide basis. While most emphasize distribution and dates of occurrence, there is some mention of habitat and natural history. For convenience they are listed by date of publication:

1912. *Michigan Bird Life,* by Walter B. Barrows. 822 pp. Michigan Agricultural College (now Michigan State Univ.), E. Lansing.

1951. *The Birds of Michigan,* by Norman A. Wood. 559 pp. The University of Michigan Press, Ann Arbor.

1959. *A Distributional Check-list of the Birds of Michigan,* by Dale A. Zimmerman and Josselyn Van Tyne. Bull. No. 608, Occasional Papers of the Museum of Zoology, The University of Michigan, Ann Arbor. 63 pp. (This is considered the current "official" list of Michigan birds, updated by the supplement in this book.)

In addition to the above, our state journal of ornithology, *The Jack-Pine Warbler,* published quarterly by our Society since 1923, publishes many articles on Michigan bird life, including all new bird records for the state. Each issue contains a seasonal survey as well as new information on bird distribution and natural history. This publication is sent free to each member of the Society.

— *The Cleveland Museum of Natural History, Wade Oval, University Circle, Cleveland, Ohio 44106.*

A Pictorial Map Guide to Birding Areas in Michigan

Legend — Map Key

▲ Michigan State Parks

⚠ Michigan State Recreation Areas

🄵 Michigan Audubon Society Sanctuaries

1. Bernard W. Baker Sanctuary
2. Voorhees Brothers Memorial Sanctuary
3. Phyllis Haehnle Memorial Sanctuary
4. Riverbank Sanctuary
5. Lew Sarett Sanctuary
6. Seven Ponds Nature Center

🔺 Some Michigan Audubon Society Campout Areas

1. Allegan Group Camp, Allegan
2. Yankee Springs Recreation Area, Middleville
3. Waterloo Recreation Area, Chelsea
4. Walden Woods, Hartland
5. Tyrone Hills, (Flint Y.M.C.A. Camp,) Fenton
6. East Tawas
7. Camp Mahn-go-tah-see, (Oakland Y.M.C.A. Camp), Hale
8. Higgins Lake Conservation School
9. Ocqueoc Lake Group Camp, Onaway

 Some Birding Areas in Michigan (After the name of the Area, the "key bird" or group of birds, are identified. In each case these are only one or several of a variety of interesting species to be found in this location.)

1. St. Joseph River (Prothonotary Warbler)
2. Lake Michigan Harbors and Coast Line (Terns)
3. Warren Woods, Portage Creek (Warblers, Shorebirds)
4. Kellogg Bird Sanctuary, Augusta (Ducks, Geese)
5. Baker Sanctuary, Marshall (Sandhill Crane)
6. Haehnle Sanctuary (Sandhill Crane)
7. North Cape, Erie (Migrants)
8. Pte. Mouillee Marsh, Monroe (Waterfowl, Wading Birds)
9. Grosse Isle, Detroit River (Whistling Swan)
10. Jack Miner's Sanctuary, Kingsville, Ontario (Geese)
11. Pt. Pelee National Park, Ontario (Migrants)
12. St. Clair Flats (Ducks)
13. "The Thumb" Farming Area (Ring-necked Pheasant)
14. Pte. Aux Barques (Knot)
15. Tawas Point (Black-bellied Plover)
16. Saginaw Bay (Herring Gull)
17. Saginaw River (Black-crowned Night Heron)
18. Shiawassee Flats (Shorebirds)
19. Central Michigan Farming Area (Turkey Vulture)
20. Muskegon Area (Bald Eagle)
21. Muskegon Bays and Shore Area (Solitary Sandpiper)
22. White River—Muskegon River Bottom Land (Prothonotary Warbler)
23. Ludington—Manistee Dunes Area (Spotted Sandpiper)
24. Upper Manistee River (Great Blue Heron)
25. Dead Stream Wilderness, Houghton Lake (Bobcat)
26. Roscommon Area (Prairie Chicken Grounds)
27. Grayling Area (Kirtland Warbler)
28. Mahn-go-tah-see Camp, Loon Lake (Common Loon)
29. Thunder Bay (Mallard Duck)
30. Thunder Bay River Basin (Red-tailed Hawk)
31. Pigeon River Elk Preserve
32. Leelanau Peninsula (Bald Eagle)
33. Grand Traverse Bay (Greater Yellowlegs)
34. Wilderness Park (Parula Warbler)
35. Beaver Island Group (Caspian Tern)
36. Straits of Mackinaw (Herring Gull)
37. Drummond Island (Sharp-tailed Grouse)
38. Whitefish Bay (Dowitcher)
39. Sleeper Lake Area, Newberry (Gray Jay)
40. Muskalonge Lake Area (Bear)
41. Tahquamenon Wilderness Area (Timber Wolf)
42. Cusino Lake Area, Shingleton (Beaver)
43. Seney National Wildlife Refuge (Canada Geese)
44. Bays De Noquet (American Merganser)
45. Presque Isle Point, Marquette (Raven)
46. Huron Mts., Big Bay (Pigeon Hawk)
47. Keweenaw Peninsula (Raven)
48. Western U.P. Farming Area (Western Meadowlark)
49. Porcupine Mts., Ontonagon (Pileated Woodpecker)
50. DeTour (Waterfowl and Shorebirds)
51. Cheboygan (Shorebirds and Warblers)
52. P. J. Hoffmaster (General)
53. P.S. Trout Fishing in Upper Michigan is Wonderful